REAL PEACE

REAL

What We Long for and Where to Find It

PEACE

A N D Y   F A R M E R

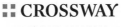

WHEATON, ILLINOIS

Library of Congress Cataloging-in-Publication Data

Farmer, Andy, 1959–
   Real peace : what we long for and where to find it / Andy Farmer.
      p. cm
   Includes bibliographical references and index.
   ISBN 978-1-4335-3529-1
   1. Peace—Religious aspects—Christianity. I. Title.
BT736.4.F37   2013
248.8'6—dc23   2012043959

Crossway is a publishing ministry of Good News Publishers.

VP		23	22	21	20	19	18	17	16	15	14	13
15	14	13	12	11	10	9	8	7	6	5	4	3	2	1

In memory of my father, Jake I. Farmer,
who taught me to honor the soldier but
love the peace that brings him home.

Contents

Acknowledgments

IT'S BEEN A PERSONALLY rewarding experience to write this book. But that experience has only been possible with the help and support of others. I would like to express my deep gratefulness to those whose help and encouragement have made this an adventure in learning and not just a project to be done.

This book would not have been written without the counsel and support of my friend and fellow pastor Dave Harvey. For close to twenty years in ministry together, he has challenged my thinking and application of truth and encouraged me to get hold of something worth writing about and then to write about it. This book simply wouldn't exist without him.

I would also like to thank the people of Covenant Fellowship Church and particularly the men on the pastoral team (past and present) who have been my friends and my community for what is now most of my life. Some of you have read and offered valuable input on these chapters. But all of you have taught me how to live out peace and nurture it in the details of life.

I'd like to thank the staff at Crossway—specifically Justin, Tara, Jill, and James—who have made the process of bringing this project into print a true joy.

There are several folks who were gracious enough to allow their stories to be woven into the content of *Real Peace*. I'm humbled by those who have been mentioned by name in the chapters for allowing me to build my thoughts with the vivid help of their experiences.

To my family—Emily and Ben, Melissa and Leo, Kelsey, Grant (and the three little ones who will wonder why Pops didn't include any pictures)—thank you for your enthusiasm for this book and for making room around our busy house for me to find peaceful places to write.

Thank you Jill, my treasure and my delight in this world and my eternal friend in the next. Everything I am or do is in some way made better by who you are in my life.

And thank you Jesus, for the peace that passes understanding, and the opportunity to share it with others.

Introduction

THE INITIAL IDEA FOR this book came to me as I stared at a picture. It wasn't a beautiful Caribbean beach scene, or a pristine Alpine meadow. It was a picture of a horse. Running. Down the homestretch of a big race. With thousands of people screaming as he churned up the track. Not exactly the idyllic scene you think would inspire a book on peace. Let me try to explain.

The horse is Secretariat, the legendary thoroughbred who won horse racing's Triple Crown in 1973. Secretariat happens to be my favorite athlete of all time, species notwithstanding. As a fourteen-year-old I somehow got caught up in the national hoopla over the Triple Crown run. I watched each race with rapt attention, spellbound by the effortless grace and power that seemed to flow out of him as he set records in the Kentucky Derby, Preakness, and Belmont Stakes.

The picture I'm referring to is a famous photo of "Big Red" closing out his Triple Crown with his historic Belmont run. My wife got it for me and had it signed by the jockey, Ron Turcotte, and the photographer who took the shot. Secretariat is running along the rail in full stride toward the finish line. But there's an odd thing about the picture. The horse and his rider are virtually alone in the shot. Secretariat won the Belmont by a mind-boggling thirty-one lengths (over eighty yards)—setting a world record for the distance that still stands. Turcotte said afterward, "I was just along for the ride." Think about it like this: with no competition and no urging from his jockey, my favorite athlete ran faster than any horse has ever run a mile and a half in history. In fact, his quarter times show that he was actually speeding up as he crossed the finish line!

I was looking at the picture one day, and I noticed something I'd never seen before. At full speed in front of thousands of people, the horse seems absolutely calm. I looked for any sign of stress and couldn't see anything. It dawned on me—he's running just for the fun of it. I was watching an animal do what he was created to do, do it with amazing beauty, and do it with what seemed like pure joy. I thought to myself, "That's peace. I need me some of that."

So I began to study the idea of peace in the Bible. In that process I discovered a second reason to write this book. I had a hard time finding anything written on peace in all its biblical aspects. I could find excellent books on our reconciliation with God through the cross, but they said very little about peace in the day-to-day experiences of life. I found some books on the experience of peace, but there wasn't much connection to the gospel in them. As I looked for helpful resources on how to do peace in the world, I found myself in the world of liberal theology, again with little if any gospel connections. I thought if I could write something that was biblical and gospel-centered, it might start conversations that don't seem to be happening much right now.

The thing that pushed me to actually do this, however, was my experience in pastoral counseling and care. As I studied peace, I became much more attuned to how people I was meeting with related to it. I began to realize that nearly everyone I talked to, regardless of their situation, was thirsting for something like peace in their lives. Whether they use the actual word or not, embedded in the language people use to describe their life struggles is a desperate cry for peace. This is abundantly obvious with the people I talk to who don't claim a saving relationship with Jesus Christ. Even among Christians who are not in difficult struggles, the lack of peace is real. I had a friend ask me today what I was writing on, and when I told her it was peace, she simply sighed, "Ahh . . . I'd love that."

That's my hope in writing this book. That you'll learn to love peace like I'm learning to love peace. Peace in all its dimensions. Let me offer some tips on how to read this book. My best suggestion is to start at the beginning; that's how I wrote it. But you could also look through the table of contents for a chapter that might speak to your immediate sense of need. You'll find application for peace in the normal stress of life (chap. 4) and also for some difficult struggles like anxiety, grief, depression, and conflict (chaps. 5–8). My hope is that if you get something out of one of those chapters, you might then want to read from the beginning.

Nearly every New Testament letter begins with a greeting that includes a blessing of peace.[1] As you begin this book, let me extend that blessing as well. May you read and be enriched with peace. Like my favorite athlete, may we learn how to run our races at peace, finding unexpected joy in doing what we were created and redeemed to do. Or as the New Testament authors tend to say it, "May grace and peace be multiplied to you" (2 Pet. 1:2), through what you read in the pages to come.

Peace, and the Problem with It

DO YOU EVER HAVE moments in life when everything seems right? I experienced one of those moments, sitting alone on a virtually deserted beach in the Outer Banks of North Carolina. It was the end of the afternoon on a cloudless day—my favorite time to be on the beach. I gazed out toward sets of curling waves coming in from an endless horizon. Rays from the late summer sun bouncing off the ocean cast the water in a metallic blue sheen. There was just enough breeze to fill my senses with the aroma of the ocean, which is to me always the aroma of vacation. I had nowhere to go, no one to talk to, nothing to do but sit and enjoy the solitude. And let my mind drift on the gentle tide of peace.

Somewhere in my tranquil mental meanderings the thought came: "This is almost perfect. But what if I were in Maui?" Now, I've never been to Maui, but I have to think it's just a little better than the barrier islands of North Carolina. I've been told that there are no bugs on the beach in Maui—which reminded me that in a little while hordes of mosquitoes would be descending on me. Tiki huts with refreshing fruit drinks (which I suppose dot the Maui beach) were nowhere to be seen. I imagined that the sand in Maui didn't stick to your feet like it does on the Atlantic Coast. Somewhere in the mist of the surf I began to detect the distinct aroma of dead fish. Bummer.

As a rising tide of grumbling began to engulf me, I was hit by a wave of guilt. What kind of pampered American am I that I can sit here and complain about this almost perfect moment, when most of the world can't even afford to be here? Someday this is going to be nothing more than a toxic wasteland because people like me go on vacation and don't separate their trash. I'm a lousy person. Of course, being a Christian, I had to factor in the God element. Here I sit by myself with the God of the universe, the Creator of all that I'm enjoying, and he is willing to open his heart to me. Yet the only thing on my mind is the lack of a convenient Tiki bar. I'm not just a lousy human, I'm a lousy Christian too.

There was nothing left to do at that point but pick up my chair and trudge back to the house murmuring, "Man, peace is hard find."

Is peace hard to find in your world? Can you mark even a single moment in your life and say, "That was peaceful"? My guess is that a lot of people can identify with my brief encounter with peace. We have those fleeting experiences when the circumstances around us and our inner state come into an almost mystical alignment and we experience that sense of "Ah, so this is what it's meant to be." It could be fifteen minutes when the kids are actually playing nicely and we can sit and catch our breath because nothing needs to be done *right now*. Or maybe it's those glorious times at the end of school finals when the pressure is off and the next semester is still a week away. What brings peace to you? There are thousands of little moments in our lives where we taste peace. But they don't last, do they? How many times have we been in that peaceful place but couldn't enjoy it because we were preoccupied with to-dos, or frustrated by something that happened earlier that day? It seems really hard to get our moods in line with our moments. Try as we might to get things just right, we don't control the things that make for peace. We don't control the weather, the traffic, flu season, sibling rivalry, lost wallets, cancelled flights, bosses that need "one more thing before you take off." Life seems to work against any sustained sense of order and tranquility. Peace is hard to find.

That's why I'm writing this book. I believe we have a peace problem. But the problem is felt much deeper than simply the limits of vacations to deliver as hoped. As a pastor I am dealing daily with people in profound life struggles. Marriages can become pitched battles of bitterness. Families are in chaos as teens and parents push each other to the brink of open hostility, and beyond. Men and women fall into gaping wells of depression. Some live in the hopeless grip of grief. Fears torment people in the sleepless shadows of night. As I have counseled and talked to people over the years, every struggle I've seen seems to contain one common problem: the absence, or loss, of peace.

That peace is hard to find shouldn't be a surprise. Peace is *the* elusive human goal. Isn't that what religion is for? To believe and practice religion faithfully is to pursue and hope to achieve whatever form of peace a particular religious tradition holds out— whether it be an inner tranquility, a oneness with the universe, a higher state, or a divine reward. But religion doesn't hold the patent on peace. Every secular utopia has had as its end goal a society of peace. People say that what the world needs is love. But why do we need love? Because if we love each other, we can all have peace. As important as love is, the end goal is peace.

Maybe the great futility of the human condition is that the thing that has been most sought after has been least experienced. In fact, the common denominator of all cultures throughout time is not the experience of peace but the reality of war. It would be safe to say there has never been a day in human history where world peace has truly been found. Somewhere in the world, there is conflict going on; it's always been that way. It has been well observed: Peace is that brief glorious moment when everybody stands around reloading.

What can be said of societies and cultures can be said of individuals as well. No person has made it through life fully at peace with himself or others. I'll talk about why later. Even those we generally cede to have found peace, the Francis of Assisis and Gandhis and Mother Theresas of the world, have been acutely aware of the inner turmoil of their souls. They viewed themselves as pursuers of peace, not possessors of it. There is a universal human quest for peace and a universal human failure to find it. And this begs the question, what really is peace? And why is it so hard to find?

Peace, and the Problem with It

If you check out the dictionary, you'll see that peace is generally defined as an absence of conflict, more specifically an absence of war. In other words, it is known by what it isn't. So, dictionarially speaking, if you are not currently in an Apache helicopter dodging RPGs, you're supposedly at peace. Enjoy!

But the absence of active war in our immediate surroundings doesn't mean we have found peace. Life is full of relational conflicts, racial and ethnic tensions, hurtful misunderstandings, and injustices against us. Then there are just the day-to-day irritations of living around other people who don't understand that their greatest joy in life should be valuing our personal space. Even if we get some momentary cooperation with our fellow man, there is enough chaos within us to make life feel like war.

Try this experiment. Google "psychological peace." Then Google "mental peace." Now, "psychological" and "mental" are generally synonymous in our language. Psychological health and mental health are two ways of talking about the same thing. But if you Google psychological peace and then mental peace, you'll find few, if any, common hits. "Psychological peace" will put you into the world of peace psychology, an academic discipline that has to do with how people cope with violence and war. Your search on mental peace will drop you into New Age and all manner of Eastern and quasimystical life paths. The definition of peace even defies the Internet.

What is peace, practically speaking? Let me give you some contrasts that seem to make up the common range of what we mean when we say the word *peace*.

Harmony rather than hostility. One of the most common words used to describe the positive aspect of peace is *harmony*. It's a great word, because harmony implies that there are different things that could function separately, but all are made better because they are together. Musical harmony is multiple notes played together in a chord. Harmony values the individual contribution to a greater whole. There is something about things working together for the benefit of all that seems like peace.

But harmony isn't the norm in life. We live in a hostile world. Things tend to grind against each other. Schedules work against spontaneity. Plaids work against stripes. Progress works against nature. Diversity works against unity. Power works against justice.

The American Deep South of the early nineteenth century was a remarkably stable culture. There was a simple reason for it. There were slaves and nonslaves. But that is not social harmony. There is no peace in stability imposed by racial or ethnic tyranny. I grew up in the Deep South during the civil rights era as a dominant culture white kid. On the surface we were not racists. But we lived in the dying throes of legal racial segregation. In many ways I was oblivious to the deep hostility that racial subjugation had produced. White people had peace with black people because we had our place and our stuff and they had their place and their stuff. But I gradually learned that segregation was not peace producing— especially if our place and stuff were nicer, and better maintained and more accessible than black people's stuff. What I learned to appreciate about Dr. Martin Luther King was his extraordinary vision of peace. He knew that simply changing the status quo wouldn't produce peace. He saw the moral need for justice for the oppressed. He called the country to account for its own laws and documents that guaranteed equality and opportunity for all people. But his vision of peace moved beyond the righting of wrongs to a society where hostility itself would crumble under the hammering of justice. King fought for justice and equality, but his dream was for a unity amid diversity that justice and equality could achieve.

Something in us loves harmony and wants to strive for it. Harmony defies the great barriers to peace: hostility, isolation, and subjugation. Harmony values the individual contribution and the unity of the whole at the same time. Harmony happens when members of a team make their highest goal the success of the team, whether that's on the field or in the factory. We taste harmony when our families all pitch in to clean out the garage and no one complains. Harmony is the resonant chord of peace in our souls.

Order rather than chaos. Keeping with the musical metaphor, my wife and I went to the orchestra a while back. The concert hall in Philadelphia, the city where we live, has an affordable section of seats behind the orchestra. So that's where we sat. I ended up really enjoying the seats because we got to see things that the normal concert goers don't see. For example, we got to see the conductor's face as he led the orchestra. I couldn't hear any mistakes in the playing, but I could tell when they happened because of the evil-eye stare the conductor would shoot at an unfortunate musician from time to time. Using opera glasses enabled me to look at the actual scores on the music stands. Sometimes I could even follow the notes as a musician was playing them.

The orchestra debuted a new concerto by a contemporary composer that could generously be called "dissonant." I don't mind some tension in music, but this piece sounded like a twenty-minute slow-motion car wreck. I got bored, so I began to survey the stage with my binoculars. I noticed one music stand with what seemed to be a blank page of music. (I've learned that this means that it's break time for the musician until the next movement.) At the top of the page was printed, "page intentionally left blank." Scribbled onto the page by the musician was the comment "like the composer's brain." I now like classical music much better.

It turns out that this piece was not really bad. It was intentionally chaotic. It was the composer's intent to create something that disrupted the sensibilities of the audience and the orchestra—to disturb the peace. Appreciating any unfamiliar art will require the disturbance of our comfortable perspective. Some art is intentionally chaotic. In this sense it portrays unsettling realities and provokes uncomfortable emotions. That doesn't mean it has to be pornographic or vulgar in its content. In fact, the art that best unsettles our sense of order usually does it in ways we can't describe. It gets under our skin, or in our ears and eyes, and pries open the Tupperware lids of our airtight worldview. It confronts us with chaos.

But we can't live like that. We're not wired for chaos. Those who seek to live for chaos flame out in it. They lose their moral and relational bearings. We survive in life by ordering it. Even artists who depict chaos consider order. They take images, materials, and ideas and arrange them in an order with the intent of upsetting our order. But art couldn't do that to us if we didn't value order in the first place. Order in the best sense of the word means security and continuity. It allows us to place trust in something today that we can be confident will be trustworthy tomorrow. Not all of us pursue order the same way. Some folks have a place for everything and everything in its place. Others get along fine with, "If I need it, I know how to find it." But look closely at anyone's life, and you'll find habits, routines, and systems that bring order out of chaos and provide a sense of peace.

Fullness rather than emptiness. What interrupted my sense of peace in the Outer Banks was an awareness that I lacked something. I lacked Maui. To have peace means that we can't have a sense of lack. To put it positively, it means we have to be full. Not full as in "stuffed," but full as in, "I'm not aware of anything that I don't have that would improve what I do have."

Think about this for a second. What would a truly full life, in the best sense of the word, mean for you? Let me take a stab at it for myself. A full life would mean that I have things in balance. It would mean that I have a house that is big enough and nice enough to really enjoy, but that I don't have to spend all my time and money trying to keep it nice. In my relationships fullness would mean that I have enough close friends that I never feel lonely or misunderstood, but not so many relationships that I feel guilty because I can't keep up with everybody. A full day would include waking up after a great night's sleep and looking ahead to being busy, but never being stressed out. I would be productive with my time, but also enjoy what I was doing. At the end of the day I would feel a sense of satisfaction that what I did that day counted for something beyond just toil. I could rest that night happy with myself. And I would look into the future with confidence that the days to come wouldn't just be same old, same old. There would be new adventures to experience, new sensations to be felt, new knowledge to obtain. I would be growing like a tree grows, never weak, always getting stronger.

But fullness is elusive. In one sense I wake up every morning wanting to be full, but having a chronic awareness of emptiness. I have a good house, but it needs work, and I am not particularly good at the work it needs. I have lots of friends, but they don't always understand me the way I want to be understood; and I have a sneaking suspicion that they don't appreciate me the way I want to be appreciated. I wake up in the morning earlier than I'd like because I tend to stay up longer than I should. I have the greatest job in the world, but stress is a daily part of it. Life is busy and complicated, and I'm running way behind. The future? The only thing I know is that I'm growing older, slower, less attractive, and less able to do things that I used to do without thinking, stretching, or medicating beforehand.

Now, I would put myself in the "more full than empty" category. But I know that isn't the experience of most people. The world is filled with emptiness. Most people around the globe have no hope of ever attaining the basic food, freedom, health, and opportunity that I take for granted. I know this. Even in my affluent culture there is alarming physical poverty. Among the haves like me, there is still pervasive poverty of hope, of meaning, and of soul.

True peace can't be compatible with a sense of emptiness. You won't be able to say, "I have peace, but what I really need is . . ." With peace comes fullness.

Settling for Peace Substitutes

In words like *harmony*, *order*, and *fullness* I've tried to capture what most people want when they say they want peace. If somebody offered you a free week of harmony, order, and fullness, would you take it? Would there be anything else you would need during that week? Chances are you can't picture what a week like that would feel like. Peace is something we've learned not to expect in life. So we learn to settle for substitutes, knock-off versions that give us the illusion that we have the real thing.

If we can't have harmony, we'll settle for tolerance. One of the words you'll hear whenever the issue of social relationships comes up these days is *tolerance*. There are tolerance policies in the workplace. Children are taught the necessity of tolerance toward their classmates. Tolerance is the way people who don't naturally get along find a way to coexist. When tolerance is used in a technical sense, it addresses how much variation between opposing things is permissible before problems happen. Tolerance means by definition that true harmony is not possible. Culturally speaking, tolerance is what happens when everything and everyone has to be equal all the time. We have to tolerate our differences, not reconcile them or harmonize them. In a tolerant society we give each other space—to a limit. But the best tolerance can do is keep tension at manageable levels. It will never deliver harmony.

For a period of my life following college, I worked in a department with two other people, a radical feminist and a gay man. They knew I was a Christian, and I don't think they knew what to do with me. As the new guy I tried to fit in as best I could, but it was obvious I didn't fit their familiar categories. In order to preserve a productive work environment, I think they chose a tolerance policy toward me as a person. Tolerance avoided the uncomfortable differences between us. But their tolerance ultimately felt patronizing and demeaning to me. I would have preferred they say they didn't really agree with what "people like me" stood for. At least I would have had the opportunity to try to express myself in ways they could understand, and they could have done the same with me. To be honest, I think I was OK settling for tolerance myself. Tolerance preserved a comfortable status quo. We were able to work with relative cooperation on a superficial level, as long as we didn't talk about our differences. I don't think any of us were enriched as people by the self-protective social walls we built in the name of tolerance.

If we can't have order, we'll wrestle for control. Here is something funny about people. We live in a world we can't control and then spend all our lives trying to tame it or keep it from taming us. There's a word for that—futility. Futility is believing we can control uncontrollable things. My favorite expression for futility is "herding cats." If you've never noticed, cats don't do herds. Just for fun I tried herding barn cats once at my parents' farm. It doesn't work—I know they're smart, but they just don't seem to get the whole leadership/teamwork thing. I thought I had gotten a handle on it at one point when they were in one spot in my parents' shed and there was only one way in or out. I wanted to see if I could move them all together from that spot to another spot. So I (humanely) dropped a pan on the floor behind them to see if I could scare them out in the same direction. One found the escape route and took off. But this apparently eliminated that option for two others. One shot up the side of the wall heading no place in particular. The other just ran around in circles. Conclusion? Herding cats—impossible. There are some things we just can't control.

One common tendency I come across in people I counsel is a craving for control. Angry people are angry because they can't control people and circumstances around them. Fearful people are fearful because things around them are constantly exerting controlling pressure on them. Lazy people and escapist people are doing all they can to avoid things that try to control them. Obsessive people are consumed with trying to manage or clean things that won't stay managed or clean. We spend life herding any cats within reach and then wonder why we're stressing and freaking out with the effort. We've bought into the illusion of control. And there's no peace in that.

If we can't have fullness, we'll pursue indulgence. My wife Jill and I have realized over the years that "dinner dates" aren't our thing. It's not because we don't love good food. In fact, dinner dates are a problem because we love good food too much. When we go to a nice restaurant, we have no self control. Everything on the menu looks good, so we order way too much. We inhale bread and salad like black holes inhale galaxies. Stimulating conversation over carefully timed courses of a meal? No time—waiter, can't you see my plate's empty? By the time we get to dessert, we don't even want it, but let's get two. We're home from our dinner date in about an hour, stuffed beyond any capacity to function as a romantic couple, good only for the couch and a movie.

I don't think that's the intent of a good restaurant experience. To do it right is to experience fullness, not (in Jill's lingo) "bloatation."

If I'm brutally honest, I can take my tendencies with restaurants and see them play out all over my life. Enough is never really enough when more is possible. The way I express myself is through how I indulge and what I consume. I don't think I'm alone in this. During the economic downturn that began in 2008, Congress passed a stimulus package directed at jumpstarting the economy. Republican Leader John Boehner lauded the passage of the bill with these patriotic words: "The sooner we get this relief in the hands of the American people, the sooner they can begin to do their job of being good consumers."[1]

Apparently, to be an American is to be a good consumer. But what makes a good consumer? Indulgence. Indulgence is the refusal to live with just enough. I can't just have all my favorite classic rock artists on my MP3 player. I need their entire catalogs, including all the tracks that weren't worth releasing back when the original album came out. But I don't just need more, I need new . . . and special . . . and . . . deluxe . . . and customized. Why? Recent psychological studies show that people who struggle with a lack of self-esteem or a sense of powerlessness tend to bolster themselves by purchasing things that give them a feeling that they are better than they feel.[2] The popular term for this is *retail therapy*, and it highlights the snare of indulgence. Indulgence isn't about enjoying what we have; it is about the obsession with what we don't have. When indulgence drives us, we will never experience fullness. No matter what we get, there is an insatiable craving for more.

Tolerance rather than harmony. Control rather than order. Indulgence rather than fullness. The goal of this book is to help us move away from whatever we depend on in life to make up for the peace we lack. But we need some basic comprehension of peace that can satisfy us enough to seek it. And as we've seen in this chapter, that isn't a simple task.

Is Peace Possible? The Experts Weigh In

In the interest of thorough research, I took some time to look up what really wise and smart people have said about peace. Using actual quotes found on relatively reliable websites, I pulled together a virtual think tank to get some answers. Let me set the imaginary scene.

We're on the beach in the Outer Banks. Buddha and the Dalai Lama are sitting under a big umbrella with their feet buried in the sand. Abe Lincoln stares intently at the line of his fishing pole for any sign of a bite. Mother Theresa is collecting seashells. Eleanor Roosevelt and Ralph Waldo Emerson are building sand castles, but Ben Franklin keeps knocking them over as he tries to get his kite in the air. John Lennon tries to teach Gandhi a basic blues pattern on his guitar. Thomas à Kempis just stares out toward the ocean at nothing in particular. From my comfortable beach chair in the midst, I start the debate.

Me: Okay, all you smart and wise guys, here's the question. How do I find peace?

Ralph Waldo Emerson: Nothing can bring you peace but yourself.

Me: Great. Everyone agree?

Buddha (objecting): There is no blissful peace until one passes beyond the agony of life and death.

Me: That's depressing.

Mother Theresa (soothingly): Peace begins with a smile.

The Dalai Lama: If you wish to experience peace, provide peace for another.

Me: Excellent, so how do I do that?

Thomas à Kempis: First, keep the peace within yourself, then you can also bring peace to others.

Me: OK, I'm confused. What comes first—peace within or peace with others?

Buddha (again): Peace comes from within, do not seek it without.

Me: Hey, Mr. Buddha, I thought you just said you can't have peace in this life? Now you say you can. Can you make up your mind?

Eleanor Roosevelt (impatiently): It isn't enough to talk about peace. One must believe in it. And it isn't enough to believe in it. One must work at it.

Me: I get it. Like you're doing with that sand castle. So how do I work at it?

John Lennon: If everyone demanded peace instead of another television set, then there'd be peace.

Benjamin Franklin (glaring at Lennon): Even peace may be purchased at too high a cost.

Me (fist-bumping BF): I totally agree. Is there any way to find peace that doesn't cost me my TV?

Abraham Lincoln: Avoid popularity if you would have peace.

Me: I'm good at that!

Mahatma Gandhi (interrupting, and just a little irritated): For peace to be real, it must be unaffected by outside circumstances.

Me (exasperated): So can somebody summarize what you're trying to tell me?!

Lennon: All we are saying is give peace a chance.

With that the whole group breaks out in song,

"Let there be peace on earth, and let it begin with me . . ."

As they break into harmonies, I pick up my chair and leave the beach. Man, peace is hard to find.

Is True Peace Possible?

I SAT IN MY office with Susan, a woman in her midthirties whom I had just met. Her face showed lines of worry; her eyes spoke of a life of sleepless nights. She described a marriage to a husband suffering with a history of mental illness. His increasing instability and erratic behavior had ruined their finances and raised concerns about his safety and hers. He would disappear for days on end with no answer for his whereabouts when he returned. He refused to take medications provided for him or see his doctor.

A friend who had brought her to church recommended she talk with me. It didn't take much conversation to realize that one thing she wasn't lacking was advice. Susan was getting strong but contradictory counsel from people around her. Trust God . . . tough love . . . protect yourself . . . submit . . . get out while you can. However, it seemed that nobody had bothered to ask her the obvious question: What did *she* want? So I thought I would.

"All I want is peace!"

One of the reasons I'm writing this book is, in that moment with Susan, I didn't know what to say next.

In the first chapter we talked about our common desire for some experience of peace. But the peace we want must be understood in real-life terms. In this chapter we're going to try to define peace. And then we'll talk about how to get it.

The Peace Conundrum

The Chinese symbol for peace represents a woman sitting under a roof, or in a home. It is a beautiful image of unthreatened vulnerability—an inner calm and outer tranquility that express peace. This was not the image of Susan's life. Susan was a vulnerable woman with no sense of security or tranquility. She was right to want peace.

But the advice she was getting was confusing. Some thought she simply needed to rid herself of the external threat to her security—her troubled husband—and she would find peace. But Susan couldn't bring herself to abandon her husband in his time of desperate need. Others encouraged her to find inner peace so she could cope with her difficult life. Susan found herself confronted with a fundamental peace problem. The question is, what comes first? Do people need to cultivate an inner tranquility that will give them peace in the turbulence of life? Or do we need to do whatever it takes to find a space for ourselves so we can have some peace? This is the conundrum that has fascinated spiritual thinkers and philosophers throughout history and across cultures. But to Susan it was the defining issue of her life.

What Is Real Peace?

There is an ancient word from the Middle East that captures the essence of this idea of peace we've been wrestling with. In Arabic it is *salaam*. In Hebrew it is *shalom*. Salaam/shalom includes both inner calm and outer tranquility. But it is far more than that. The range of meaning includes order, security, relational harmony, well-being, wholeness, and a sense of flourishing life. As one author has simply put it, "Shalom, in other words, is the way things ought to be."[1]

"The way things ought to be." That sounds good. But according to whom? According to me? According to you? What if your "way things ought to be" is different from mine? And what if my "way things ought to be" can't happen if yours does? Who gets shalom and who doesn't? Isn't that how wars and racial and ethnic conflicts happen in the first place? My country or people say the way things ought to be requires us to have what you've got. Whoever wins the war gets the shalom. Is that real peace?

If real peace is possible, it can't be something we create. So who determines shalom? Simply put, God does. The idea of shalom is uniquely God-centered. In other words, shalom is not something that can exist on its own in this world. It is a gift from God into human experience. Even more, it is the effect on human experience when life is lived the way God designed it to be lived. Behind "the way things ought to be" is a God who is personal and committed in his personal being to a world where peace flourishes—where things are the way they ought to be in his eyes.

Now, if you've been reading along with me up to this point and find that my dropping into God-language is not really where you want this to go, I understand. As you'll see in the next chapter, it isn't where I always have gone, either. But I do think that a God-centered peace story is worth considering. It's a fascinating story as well.

The Beginning of Peace

The opening pages of the Bible reveal that God has woven peace into the very fabric of existence. The creation story in Genesis is a beautiful poetic depiction of the origin and meaning of everything comprehensible to our human existence. It is a story that is meant to draw us to wonder and worship that a God beyond time and space could create and rule over something so magnificent as the cosmos. The poem moves from the utter simplicity of verse 1—"In the beginning, God created the heavens and the earth"—through an escalation of images and symbolic language to the pinnacle act of creation—the placing of man (and woman) in their fully realized earthly habitation.

God's initial act of creation produces a cosmos "without form and void" (Gen. 1:2). What verse 2 describes is desolation and chaos and uninhabitability. It is the raw material for something else God intends. And so begins the forming process. Light and dark, earth and sky, land and waters—contrasting elements showing the Creator's artistic structuring of the basic elements in his grand design.

And then to this he begins to add life—populating the desolate expanse with flora and fauna of unique and diverse beauty. Formless and void have become harmony, order, and fullness. But the creation project is not just natural beauty. The Creator's ultimate goal for his cosmos is revealed in the creation of mankind—creatures uniquely designed to populate this natural world with enjoyers and caretakers of all that God has made.

The creation poem reveals the grand design and activity of God. Though completely at peace within himself, God acts by creative word to give life to beings uniquely designed to comprehend and display his glory. And he places these beings in a perfect environment for that purpose. In that environment, that garden of delights, that Eden (Gen. 2:8), they are to live in joyous dependence on him, in humble wonder at all he has given them in creation, and in loving cooperation with each other in the stewardship of it all. Shalom is the lifestyle, the culture, the politics of Eden. As author Tim Keller describes it,

> God created all things to be in a beautiful, harmonious, interdependent, knitted, webbed relationship to one another. Just as rightly related physical elements form a cosmos or a tapestry, so rightly related human beings form a community. This interwovenness is what the Bible calls shalom, or harmonious peace.[2]

What we see in Eden, in other words, is life "the way it ought to be."

What Happened to Shalom?

However, as we've already seen in chapter 1, peace is not our normal experience. What we experience of shalom is vaporous, fleeting. Harmony gives way to hostility, order to chaos, and fullness to emptiness. For many of us, like Susan above, peace is a pipe dream, swallowed up by a life of strife without and within. What happened to shalom? Where did it go? Can we get it back?

In Genesis 3 the poetry of creation abruptly ends with the tragedy of the fall. The particulars of the story are commonly known. Adam and Eve are in the garden at peace. The Serpent (the Deceiver) enters their existence with his own power agenda and the political propaganda to sell it: his take is that this rule of God's shalom is really a rule of oppression. God the Creator is not the provider of all good things; he is the withholder of the one essential thing, the right to live on our own terms. The Deceiver invites Eve, and through her, Adam, into rebellion against their Creator and Sustainer. Enticed and inflamed by desire for the one thing God will not allow them to have, Adam and Eve knowingly and willfully reject the way things ought to be for the way they want things to be. Shalom between the Creator and his favored creature is broken.

Adam and Eve have forsaken their peace with God and have aligned themselves with God's enemy. The consequences are profound. There will be no peace in their lives. Harmony? They will be at war with the Deceiver (Gen. 3:15) and in perpetual strife with each other (3:16). Order? They will now live in frustration with their environment (3:17). Fullness? They are driven out of the garden of delight (3:24). Most profoundly, however, the relationship of creature and Creator is forever changed. In this separation there can be no shalom. Because now God has himself become their enemy. And because he is their enemy, he is ours as well.

Dutch theologian Herman Bavinck wrote,

> For if the history of the world clearly teaches us anything, it is this: that God has a quarrel with His creature. There is disagreement, separation, conflict between God and His world. God does not agree with man, and man does not agree with God. Each goes his own way, and each has his own idea and will about things.[3]

At war with God. It is an essential but very uncomfortable biblical truth to wrap our brains around. When we talk about Genesis 3, we talk about "the fall" of humanity in sin. But the way we talk about our sinful condition before God tends to sound passive. Something bad happened, and we have to live with the lousy reality of it. We talk about "not knowing God" and of "being lost." We may even talk about being "dead to God" or "dead in sin." We need God to "save" us because we need saving. We want God to heal us because we're broken. God is in the business of finding people who are lost, and giving new life. All of these are true and essential biblical metaphors, but there is a reality to our state that cannot be stomached easily. To be an enemy of God is not a passive state.

The state of war between the Creator and his creatures is called, in theological terms, *enmity*. The book of Genesis plays this enmity out in the petulant rage of Cain (chap. 4), the sorry rebellion of humankind leading to the flood (chap. 6), and the absurd power play of the Tower of Babel (chap. 11). Were you to treat the Old Testament as simply an account of the religious beliefs and practices of ancient people, you would have a very depressing story. The moral of the book would be, "If God is your enemy, you haven't got a prayer."

Is the idea of God as our enemy uncomfortable for you to consider? It should be. But it is a pervasively human truth, hard as we try to move beyond it. The history of religion is a history of people trying to appease whatever deity has arisen in their culture. We are a species that lives with the sense that we are being watched by someone or something larger than we are, and that someone or something isn't happy with us. So we sacrifice and we atone and, in frustration, we shake our fists at gods who are never satisfied with what we try to do to get on their good side. The enmity problem isn't just something that people who believe in a personal God struggle with. A large psychological study on religious anger published in January 2011 found that people who don't have a belief in a personal God (atheists, agnostics, Eastern religions) actually tend to have a higher struggle with anger against God than God-believing people.[4] Apparently you don't have to believe in God to be ticked off with him.

Maybe you have never thought about God this way. For many God is "the Man upstairs" who's OK with us if we're OK with him. I had a philosophy professor in college who told me that arguing with God is what God expects of thinking people. But God doesn't seem to see it that way. Twentieth-century preacher D. Martyn Lloyd-Jones sums up the problem of enmity with God well:

> Man has turned his back upon God and has enmity in his heart towards God and is trying to live his life in this world without God and apart from God, and he regards God as one who interferes and upsets everything. . . . And of course you find this great story unfolded in the pages of the Bible and it is the whole key to the understanding of secular history, man fighting God, man refusing to humble himself before God, and arrogantly and proudly doing the exact opposite, so that what you have in the Bible is an account of the conflict between this glorious God and man in sin.[5]

Maybe the most bold-faced description of enmity comes in a phrase repeated multiple times by the prophet Isaiah: "'There is no peace,' says the Lord, 'for the wicked'" (48:22; see 57:21).

If we are a race at enmity with God, then one thing is certain. We are fighting a war that we cannot win. We are in a place we were never intended to be—God is on our bad side and we are on his. And life at enmity with God, frankly, stinks. Keller says,

> When we lost our relationship with God, the whole world stopped "working right." The world is filled with hunger, sickness, aging, and physical death. Because our relationship with God has broken down, shalom is gone—spiritually, psychologically, socially, and physically.[6]

The experience of enmity, in human terms, is known as *alienation*. We are alienated from God and he from us. Alienation is the virtual opposite of shalom. Alienation is a throbbing awareness that things are not as they should be. We'll talk more about alienation in the next chapter.

Any recovery of peace must fill the dark hole of our alienation with God. Yet we are unable to do anything about it. In our natures the sinful propensities of our forbearers Adam and Eve run deep— a corruption of desire that sets every natural thought and inclination against God (Rom. 1:21). Our basic religious impulses say more about how we want to control God or barter things from him than how we want to live in the joyful satisfaction with his rule over our lives that he originally intended. This, friends, is the sorry human predicament—enmity with God and alienation in life.

God's Surprising Solution

But don't give up on the story just yet. God didn't create us for this! The Old Testament is not the brief grisly account of God squashing the pathetic and misguided rebellion of man. It is the unfolding epic of God's mercy plan for the human race. The first eleven chapters of Genesis are not the story; they are the prologue to the story. God faces down his enemies, thwarts their uprising, and then, amazingly, offers a way back to shalom. This peace plan isn't a negotiation, as if two exhausted foes agree that further hostilities are useless. We bring nothing to the table with which to bargain. God doesn't offer amnesty, simply ignoring the evil done against him. He can't overlook cosmic treason.

What God does offer is beyond comprehension. It is redemptive counterinsurgency. He launches a strategically targeted strike, not to punish, but to capture a beachhead where he can begin a work of new creation. His target is one man—Abram of the Chaldeans. The assault launches in Genesis 12.

> Now the LORD said to Abram, "Go from your country and your kindred and your father's house to the land that I will show you. And I will make of you a great nation, and I will bless you and make your name great, so that you will be a blessing. I will bless those who bless you, and him who dishonors you I will curse, and in you all the families of the earth shall be blessed." (vv. 1–3)

It is God's intent to work shalom from within the enemy camp. He will create a people from one old man, and that people will be at the center of his peace plan for the earth. God will reach his enemies through identification with them. Generation after generation God will patiently work this shalom out with man through the promises and commandments of the old covenant. It is an inexplicable commitment to tie his glory to a people whose infidelity and hard-heartedness render them virtually no different than the enemies of God around them. The promise of peace runs through the story of Abraham's descendents—the people of Israel. It connects the existence of this little Semitic tribe to the great redemptive counterinsurgency of God.

In the pages of the Old Testament we see the beginnings of the restoration of peace. God provides the law with its extensive sacrificial system to allow a channel of mercy to his people. This sacrificial system is not intended to change the hearts of people, but it does allow a way for sinful people to rightly relate to a holy God. Through the mediating sacrificial blood of innocent animals, a representative atonement for guilt and sin occurs. The power is not in these rituals, as if they can change God's posture toward sin. The power is in the condescension of God who accepts the "peace offerings" that are brought to him. The sufficiency of the sacrifices is the power of grace.

This wandering insurgency needs a base of operations. So God moves his people to a little strip of land in Palestine that even in ancient days was an unfortunate buffer zone between great warring empires. He centers his own headquarters in a little town in that strip of land known as the "place of peace"—Jeru-salem. Over centuries this people is meant to find security and to flourish as a nation in this small part of the world. And from there God's peace is to be declared.

But that never really happens. The people prove themselves to be stubbornly hard-hearted and wickedly unfaithful. They carry within them the sinful propensities of their forefathers, going back to Adam. And so they disobey God, neglect and abuse his provisions of grace, and run after the violent and perverse ways of the people around them. The peace insurgency is swallowed up in idolatry. As one theologian has put it, "Idolatry—wrongly perceiving who is in charge—is the opposite of shalom."[7] Among God's chosen people, harmony gives way to anarchy, order to chaos, and fullness to famine.

The human narrative of the Old Testament is not easy reading. It is a tragedy that plays out in excruciating detail—the epic demise of God's very people into moral depravity, subjugation, and ruination. Yes, there is a remnant preserved, and a return from exile. But there is no return to former glory, no rejuvenation of purpose—just a small, poor little people destined to be conquered and reconquered by emerging empires looking for advantageous real estate. It is left to the weeping prophet Jeremiah to lament the pitiful state of the peace project of God.

> I have become the laughingstock of all peoples,
>   the object of their taunts all day long.
> He has filled me with bitterness;
>   he has sated me with wormwood.
>
> He has made my teeth grind on gravel,
>   and made me cower in ashes;
> my soul is bereft of peace;
>   I have forgotten what happiness is;
> so I say, "My endurance has perished;
>   so has my hope from the LORD." (Lam. 3:14–18)

The Prince and the Price

Fortunately, the Old Testament is not limited to human tragedy. In fact, the great sweeping desolation of Israel is only part of a larger glorious story that God is telling. The peace insurgency isn't defeated after all. In the very midst of calamity, God calls other prophets to declare the transcendent plan of peace. Nearly all the prophets allude to this plan, but it is given to Isaiah to most expressively play it out.

The peace plan as declared by Isaiah introduces two remarkable figures into the fray. They are described but not named. God's shalom insurgency hinges on who they are and what they do. We discover the first figure in Isaiah 9:

> But there will be no gloom for her who was in anguish. In the
> former time he brought into contempt the land of Zebulun and

the land of Naphtali, but in the latter time he has made glorious
the way of the sea, the land beyond the Jordan, Galilee of the
nations.

> The people who walked in darkness
>> have seen a great light;
> those who dwelt in a land of deep darkness,
>> on them has light shone.
> You have multiplied the nation;
>> you have increased its joy;
> they rejoice before you
>> as with joy at the harvest,
>> as they are glad when they divide the spoil.
> For the yoke of his burden,
>> and the staff for his shoulder,
>> the rod of his oppressor,
>> you have broken as on the day of Midian.
> For every boot of the tramping warrior in battle tumult
>> and every garment rolled in blood
>> will be burned as fuel for the fire.
> For to us a child is born,
>> to us a son is given;
> and the government shall be upon his shoulder,
>> and his name shall be called
> Wonderful Counselor, Mighty God,
>> Everlasting Father, Prince of Peace.
> Of the increase of his government and of peace
>> there will be no end,
> on the throne of David and over his kingdom,
>> to establish it and to uphold it
> with justice and with righteousness
>> from this time forth and forevermore.
> The zeal of the Lord of hosts will do this. (vv. 1–7)

What an amazing promise! Isaiah envisions the darkness to
come and pronounces light! Order, harmony, and fullness will be
restored in a new and abundantly rich nation of God. But there is
far more here than anyone can imagine. God's peace insurgency
will not only survive, it will reign in the earth. It will reign because
God himself will make it so. Peace will be the government of God.

A child is born, a Son is given, and he will be the Prince of Peace. What do we know about this Prince of Peace? It appears that he will arise from the unlikely regions of Galilee. He will rule in the royal line of David—the king of Israel's kings. But he will represent God like no other human can represent God. He will break the yoke of human oppression and bring light to a world of darkness. He will rule with justice and righteousness. And of the increase of his government and peace there will be no end—in expanse or duration. His kingdom will have cosmic scope and eternal security.

But how will this be accomplished? Who is that man who can take this peace insurgency and build it into an empire? What leadership and force must be exerted to build an everlasting nation? How can this great peace be won? The answer comes in the introduction of the other figure later in Isaiah's prophecy:

> Behold my servant, whom I uphold,
>   my chosen, in whom my soul delights;
> I have put my Spirit upon him;
>   he will bring forth justice to the nations.
> He will not cry aloud or lift up his voice,
>   or make it heard in the street;
> a bruised reed he will not break,
>   and a faintly burning wick he will not quench;
>   he will faithfully bring forth justice.
> He will not grow faint or be discouraged
>   till he has established justice in the earth;
>   and the coastlands wait for his law. (42:1–4)

There is no grand title for this figure. He is simply "my servant." He is identified with the people of God, but his calling extends beyond them. The Servant will bring forth the just reign of God throughout the nations in the power of the Spirit of God. He will not come to exact vengeance—his means of conquest will leave no destruction in its wake. Somehow the counterinsurgency of God will become the reign of God. But how can this happen? Isaiah now pulls back the veil and reveals the unimaginable plan of peace. Read this slowly in light of the story we've been following:

Who has believed what he has heard from us?
  And to whom has the arm of the LORD been revealed?
For he grew up before him like a young plant,
  and like a root out of dry ground;
he had no form or majesty that we should look at him,
  and no beauty that we should desire him.
He was despised and rejected by men;
  a man of sorrows, and acquainted with grief;
and as one from whom men hide their faces
  he was despised, and we esteemed him not.

Surely he has borne our griefs
  and carried our sorrows;
yet we esteemed him stricken,
  smitten by God, and afflicted.
But he was pierced for our transgressions;
  he was crushed for our iniquities;
upon him was the chastisement that brought us peace,
  and with his wounds we are healed.
All we like sheep have gone astray;
  we have turned—every one—to his own way;
and the LORD has laid on him
  the iniquity of us all.

He was oppressed, and he was afflicted,
  yet he opened not his mouth;
like a lamb that is led to the slaughter,
  and like a sheep that before its shearers is silent,
  so he opened not his mouth.
By oppression and judgment he was taken away;
  and as for his generation, who considered
that he was cut off out of the land of the living,
  stricken for the transgression of my people?
And they made his grave with the wicked
  and with a rich man in his death,
although he had done no violence,
  and there was no deceit in his mouth.

Yet it was the will of the LORD to crush him;
  he has put him to grief;
when his soul makes an offering for guilt,

> he shall see his offspring; he shall prolong his days;
> the will of the LORD shall prosper in his hand.
> Out of the anguish of his soul he shall see and be satisfied;
> by his knowledge shall the righteous one, my servant,
>   make many to be accounted righteous,
>   and he shall bear their iniquities.
> Therefore I will divide him a portion with the many,
>   and he shall divide the spoil with the strong,
> because he poured out his soul to death
>   and was numbered with the transgressors;
> yet he bore the sin of many,
>   and makes intercession for the transgressors. (53:1–12)

It is here where we must stop and open our minds to what has really happened. The counterinsurgency of God is the death of God! Isaiah 53 is a chapter that has never fit any materialistic interpretation of the Bible. Commentator John Bright wrote, "No concept in the entire Old Testament is stranger, more elusive or more movingly profound than this."[8] It gives no hope to religious people. It gives no hope to secular people. But if there is truly a state called peace to be experienced in this life, Isaiah 53 holds the key. Remember what we said earlier. Sin has created enmity between man and God. The only way to resolve that enmity is through judgment for sin. In Isaiah 53, judgment thunders down. The Servant is chosen by God. Yet he is despised and rejected. He is slaughtered for something that he did not do—an innocent condemned as guilty. But he is no hero or martyr. His death accomplishes something no other death could accomplish. He bears our sins and carries our sorrows; he takes our transgressions upon himself—he himself becomes the peace offering for our sin that pleases the divine Judge. And he does this willingly, actively, and joyfully. What does his death do? Look carefully at verse 5:

> But he was pierced for our transgressions;
>   he was crushed for our iniquities;
> upon him was the chastisement that brought us peace,
>   and with his wounds we are healed.

Isaiah offers us the answer to the problem of peace in two remarkable figures. The Prince of Peace, whose reign of peace will never end, is one. He is not simply a representative of God—he is "Mighty God . . . Prince of Peace" (Isa. 9:6). He alone has the authority to offer peace to God's enemies. And the Suffering Servant, who could only bear our sorrows and griefs and be crushed for our iniquities if he had none of his own, is the other. The only one who has no grief and has no transgression is God himself. The astounding answer to the problem of peace is that the Prince of Peace who offers peace and the Suffering Servant who paid the price of peace are the same. The substitutionary death of the divine Prince of Peace brought us peace. God has reconciled us to himself through his own divine self-sacrifice.

The Person of Peace

We've covered a lot of ground in this chapter. It's some heady stuff. But I can summarize it pretty succinctly. We want peace. Really, we need peace, because we are alienated from the one source of true peace in the cosmos—our Creator God. And peace has come through the intervention of God in his own self-sacrifice—a divine atonement—that resolves the enmity between us and God. But what does that mean for the dear woman who desperately wants peace in her troubled life? What does it mean for me, and for you? To explore that, we need to talk about the Servant Prince of Peace. We need to talk about Jesus Christ.

3

The Prince of Peace

IN CHAPTER 2 WE COVERED the grand sweep of God's peace insurgency in a world at enmity with its Creator. Our story led us to the astounding conclusion that the way back to peace comes in the willing and atoning death of the Prince of Peace, Jesus Christ, for the sin of God's enemies, so that there might be reconciliation between God and the race of man. These are obviously grand truths that can be difficult to apply to our own peace struggles. In this chapter we're going to look at what the reconciliation activity of Jesus Christ has meant for us and how it can transform the way we live. But first let me introduce you to an alienated young man.

How Not to Choose a Major in College

I grew up in a church-going home, but it didn't take. Throughout high school many things mattered deeply to me—girls, music, soccer, partying, and social standing tended to vie for the top spot in my pyramid of values. But God never mattered. My only memorable religious experience occurred at an evangelistic revival I attended at a friend's request. At the end of the shouting, the vividly dressed evangelist asked anyone who knew they were a sinner to close their eyes and raise their hand. I thought, "Well the way you describe it, I seem to fit the description." The next thing I knew, I was being guided out of my seat by an usher and moved up to the front of the church where things were said and people clapped. I was then ushered into another room where a middle-aged guy sat down across the table and asked if I knew what I had just done.

All I remember was that he had really, really bad breath. Being born again didn't happen for me that night, but I've carried breath mints with me ever since. I went away to a small liberal arts college in another state. I went because they let me play collegiate soccer; my parents let me go because there was a denominational word in the name of the school. But I wasn't there too long before I realized that this was not a very religious place. The school faculty included a number of new professors who had been heavily radicalized in the 1960s. It was at this school that I heard a word that succinctly captured my experience in life: *alienation*.

Alienation isn't isolation. We can be alienated in a crowd. Alienation is the sense of detachment that says, "I'm not really essential to anything that's happening around me." Alienated people can be depressed, or angry, or apathetic—alienation doesn't have to look like anything on the outside. Some philosophers view it as the appropriate state of mind for people existing in a screwed up world—hence the "existentialist" school of philosophy.

As we've moved into what is commonly called the postmodern world, the cultural experience of alienation has changed. Through technology the world is a much smaller place. The result is an overwhelming amount of information we have to process and potential choices we have to make. The effect, according to one sociologist, is the feeling that "I'm living this life, but could have lived so many other ones."[1]

In short, in previous generations alienation was blamed on the control of one group of people over another. In the postmodern West, alienation comes because no one is in control—there is no clear way for us to make sense of the world around us and no one to blame for the problems that come our way. Different world, same problem. Alienation.

You probably wouldn't have met me back in college and said, "Wow, that guy is seriously alienated." I was superficially social and philosophically bent, and had a relatively stable sense of self-worth. But I was alienated in profound ways. "Keep yourself entertained so you don't despair" was my life coping mantra. I moved between groups of people because I didn't find any group where I felt I belonged. I was high on mistrust of people and low on confidence that the world around me was going to improve. Maybe the best way I can describe myself at the time is "jaded but distractible"—a high-functioning and easily amused form of alienation.

At this time I was introduced to the patron saint of alienation—Karl Marx. Marx was the nineteenth-century German economist/philosopher whose social theories provided the rhetoric for communism in the twentieth century. Marx made sense to me. He told me why I was alienated. He said it was the inevitable result of living in a world where what I needed in order to have meaning in life was controlled by others. Strictly speaking, he was talking about the means of production—that I was meant to find dignity and worth in what I could produce with my life. But the best I could hope for was working for someone else's enrichment.

In a larger sense, Karl Marx offered a vision of peace. According to Marx, if the fruits of production could be returned to those who do the work, then the natural state of humanity would be restored. Things would be as they ought to be. Marx worked on many levels for me. Everything that mattered to me was beyond my control. I had no idea what I wanted to do with my life. I wanted a deep and meaningful relationship with a girl, but couldn't make that happen. I quit the soccer team one year because I thought the coach was unjustly punishing me for driving seven hours each way to see a Bruce Springsteen concert the day before a big game. And then on July 15, 1979, I heard President Jimmy Carter talk about the world I was going to graduate into.

> I want to talk to you right now about a fundamental threat to American democracy. . . . I do not refer to the outward strength of America, a nation that is at peace tonight everywhere in the world, with unmatched economic power and military might. The threat is nearly invisible in ordinary ways. It is a crisis of confidence. It is a crisis that strikes at the very heart and soul and spirit of our national will. We can see this crisis in the growing doubt

about the meaning of our own lives and in the loss of a unity of purpose for our nation. . . . In a nation that was proud of hard work, strong families, close-knit communities, and our faith in God, too many of us now tend to worship self-indulgence and consumption. Human identity is no longer defined by what one does, but by what one owns. But we've discovered that owning things and consuming things does not satisfy our longing for meaning . . .[2]

While he has taken a lot of heat for this "Crisis of Confidence" speech, Carter, as history has shown, was honestly confronting some serious problems. But when even the president starts using alienation language, what's an aimless twenty-year-old supposed to do? So I became a Marxist. I chose my degree in order to "major" in Marxism. Marx gave me an odd form of purpose in life. Marx has a solution for alienation—socialist revolution. The alienation that humans experience would be set right and the peace that humanity seeks would be accomplished with the Great Revolution. That sounded cool, or at least punk, which back in the late 1970s was better than cool. So me and my fellow aspiring Marxists spent our college years sitting around listening to The Clash and talking up proletariat revolution.

Another thing Karl Marx did was free me from any remaining sense of obligation to God. It is Marx, after all, who said, "Religion is the sigh of the oppressed creature, the heart of a heartless world, and the soul of soulless conditions. It is the opium of the people."[3] It didn't take long to realize how much personal indulgence can be pursued with abandon if you don't have to factor God's ever-watching eye into the mix. We campus Marxists were a partying bunch. However, before long I began to notice that neither compelling political philosophy nor a full slate of good times was really touching our collective alienation. If anything, it was only getting worse. Our lives began to fray and break—relational chaos, emotional breakdowns, drug and alcohol addictions, even criminal convictions—among people who had every privilege we could imagine. Deep within me was a growing sense of true despair. And

I couldn't blame it on anyone or anything but me. I began to realize I was a profound fraud. There was something in me that couldn't be accounted for by society, politics, philosophy, or life experience. I carried in my soul a corruption that was pervasively influencing my thoughts and actions. It seemed evil to me. I couldn't control it. I was coming face-to-face with sin, but I didn't even believe in the God toward whom it was against.

In what I now see as the amazing providence of God, it was at this time that I encountered a small group of Christians on campus. They were nothing like me; in fact, very little they did attracted me. But they were real—who they said they were on the inside seemed to be reflected in how they lived. I was fragmented, hypocritical; they were whole and sincere. I was alienated; they were at peace.

On February 10, 1981, it all exploded for me. I was sitting in a dorm lounge with one of the Christians, having a long conversation about spiritual things. I, of course, was the principled atheist, she was the naive believer. My friend was patiently listening to hours of impassioned (but apparently unconvincing) Marxist rhetoric. Somewhere around three in the morning I apparently lectured her to sleep. I sat alone, in the dark, soundless room with my dark, godless thoughts. My life began to unravel. In that silence, I stopped thinking my thoughts and began to think thoughts that weren't my own. They were truth, vestiges and strings of childhood Bible verses that had somehow clung to a mind that had sought to purge them away. There was a palpable sense of God's presence—not god in the philosophical cage I had created, but the God who was frighteningly transcendent and engagingly close at the same time. In that moment I was aware of a call—a personal invitation to renounce everything I wanted and believed and stood for. It was as close to an audible voice as it could be without shattering the silence in the room—as close to a face-to-face encounter with God without blinding hot glory engulfing a college suite lounge. Oh, without a doubt it was Jesus Christ saying, "Forget your life. Look up to me."

I often tell people that at about 3:44 a.m. on February 10, 1981, I was an atheistic, hard-hearted sinner, destined for God's wrath and not even knowing it. At about 3:45 a.m. I was a child of God and heir with Christ. It was that powerful. And that simple. I've never looked back.

Not Revolution, but Reconciliation

I've taken time to tell my story because I think it can help us understand what God's peace plan in Jesus Christ means for our lives. You see, in that suite lounge I was truly converted and knew it, though I had very little sense of what had happened to me and what it meant for my life. But a very important passage of Scripture has helped me understand and live out the salvation I received at 3:45 a.m., 2.10.81.

In his letter to the Ephesians, the apostle Paul writes,

> Therefore remember that at one time you Gentiles in the flesh, called "the uncircumcision" by what is called the circumcision, which is made in the flesh by hands—remember that you were at that time separated from Christ, alienated from the commonwealth of Israel and strangers to the covenants of promise, having no hope and without God in the world. But now in Christ Jesus you who once were far off have been brought near by the blood of Christ. For he himself is our peace, who has made us both one and has broken down in his flesh the dividing wall of hostility by abolishing the law of commandments expressed in ordinances, that he might create in himself one new man in place of the two, so making peace, and might reconcile us both to God in one body through the cross, thereby killing the hostility. And he came and preached peace to you who were far off and peace to those who were near. For through him we both have access in one Spirit to the Father. So then you are no longer strangers and aliens, but you are fellow citizens with the saints and members of the household of God, built on the foundation of the apostles and prophets, Christ Jesus himself being the cornerstone, in whom the whole structure, being joined together, grows into a holy temple in the Lord. In him you also are being built together into a dwelling place for God by the Spirit. (Eph. 2:11–22)

Some brief context might be helpful. Chapter 1 of this letter is one of the great expositions in the New Testament of what life is meant to be for those who are "in Christ." In chapter 2 Paul sets out the gospel in one long, dramatic sentence (vv. 1–10), where he definitively asserts that salvation is by grace alone (v. 8). Beginning in verse 11 he introduces us to the amazing doctrine of reconciliation—how the death of Christ has brought us peace. Let's explore the implications of reconciliation that come from this passage.

Reconciliation Has Been Accomplished for Us by the Cross

As we talked about in the last chapter, the Old Testament hope for peace was wrapped up in the sacrificial death of the Prince of Peace. But this death could not have been simply a voluntary martyrdom. Jesus didn't come to show us how to live and die, he came to die for us. The biblical word for this is *atonement*—the payment for sin by death. It is the particular death of Jesus Christ—the Prince of Peace, the Suffering Servant—that removed the guilt of sin separating us from God, leading to reconciliation between us and God. Reconciliation is inseparable from this divine atonement. At the very center of his peace declaration in Ephesians 2, Paul writes, "But now in Christ Jesus you who once were far off have been brought near by the blood of Christ" (v. 13) and that reconciliation has come "through the cross" (v. 16). We cannot have peace without reconciliation with God. There is no way to reconciliation apart from the atoning death of Christ. Peace is atonement fruit. Paul makes this abundantly obvious in his letter to the Romans: "Therefore, since we have been justified by faith, we have peace with God through our Lord Jesus Christ . . . while we were enemies we were reconciled to God by the death of his Son . . ." (Rom. 5:1, 10). How do we know we have peace with God? Puritan John Flavel says it with poetic clarity: "Hear the voice of peace through the blood of the cross."[4]

In that early morning in 1981, my confident a-Theism was decimated by Theos himself. I made a conscious decision to believe the preposterous notion that Jesus Christ was alive and he was essential for my life. The deep jaded cynicism in my heart was gone. I felt new, and for the first time in my life, real. I wanted more than anything to follow this Jesus whom I had only known before in fragmentary stories and iconic images. However, like so many people who have powerful conversion experiences find, conversion peace, though genuine, is not the whole story.

With an awareness of the call to follow Christ came a deep sense of the cost that following would require of me. My life would have to change dramatically and irreversibly. I would have to begin proclaiming things that I had been mocking even earlier that day. There was a truckload of enjoyable behavior that would now be off-limits to me. I would probably lose my friends. I soon realized that inner peace was not always going to be the sensation of true faith.

I began to think that maybe my peace as a Christian would be determined by how well I was performing as a Christian. In pastoral ministry I regularly encounter people who struggle with this performance-based approach to faith. Their testimony is heavily colored by what they had to stop doing to start following Jesus. They live in fear that someday they may do something wrong, or fail to do something right, that will prove that the peace they thought they had was a sham, a religious high and nothing more. They never question God's ability to save, but they live with constant concern that they might just be unsavable.

Whether we look to our experience or to our performance for peace, we will never find it there. Perhaps we should take the wise advice of nineteenth-century pastor R. M. McCheyne:

> Some of you think you will come to peace by looking in to your own heart. Your eye is riveted there. You watch every change there. If you could only see a glimpse of light there, oh, what joy it would give you! If you could only see a melting of your stony heart, if you could only see your heart turning to God, if you could only see a glimpse of the image of Jesus in your heart, you would be at peace; but you cannot,—all is dark within. Oh, dear souls, it is not there you will find peace! . . . You must look to a declared Christ.[5]

This is Paul's radical declaration: "He himself is our peace" (Eph. 2:14)! Your peace is not your experience, it is not your performance. Your peace is a person—the Son of God crushed for your sin, risen for your life, reigning for your hope. He himself is the peace that has been declared to you (2:17). When you are tempted to question whether your peace is true peace from God, whether it is lasting peace, whether it is defined by your experience or determined by your performance, look to your declared Christ! As one theologian sums it up, I know I have true peace because "I have been died for."[6]

Reconciliation Restores the Harmony
That God Intended for All Relationships

A contemporary Marxist website defines alienation like this:

> Alienation is the process whereby people become foreign to the world they are living in. The concept of alienation is deeply embedded in all the great religions and social and political theories of the civilized epoch, namely, the idea that some time in the past people lived in harmony, and then there was some kind of rupture which left people feeling like foreigners in the world, but some time in the future this alienation would be overcome and humanity would again live in harmony with itself and Nature.[7]

Sound familiar? That's the same story we unpacked from the Old Testament in chapter 2. A primal harmony, cosmically ruptured, resulting in a pervasive sense of disconnection from the way things should be, a flickering hope of the restoration to a former state of order and harmony and fullness. This is the exact human condition that Paul addresses in Ephesians 2. The only difference is that Paul is describing alienation in a God-oriented world. He defines alienation in some very specific terms according to a worldview that includes two basic types of people—Gentiles and Jews. This isn't simply racial ethnic distinction. Paul's division of humanity speaks to the peace project God initiated in the Old Testament. The Jews were the people elected by God to represent his peacemaking initiative to the world. They were the ones who were marked as God's covenant people. They received the mark of covenant in circumcision, and the rites of covenant in law and promise. Gentiles are simply everyone else. Paul's audience in Ephesus is the "everyone else." Chances are, you and I are the Gentiles Paul addresses. So we should pay attention to what he says.

Paul sets reconciliation in contrasting images. We are the "uncircumcision"—we have no chosen place in God's plan in "the circumcision." We are not joined with God's commonwealth, we are strangers to it. We are not near God, we are "far off" from him. The nature of our relationship with God is hostility (Eph. 2:14, 16; the Greek word translated "hostility" is more naturally translated as "enmity," which ties us back to what we learned in the previous chapter). Because we are hostile/at enmity with God, we are also hostile/at enmity with each other. That's our alienation. It is really a far deeper problem than Marx and his other philosopher kin could possibly comprehend. Alienation at its core is "having no hope and without God in the world" (2:12).

Reconciliation is the resolution of this pervasive alienation. As we've already seen, reconciliation has come through the cross. What has the cross accomplished?

THE WAR WITH GOD IS OVER

The atoning sacrifice of Christ has reconciled us to God, "killing the hostility [enmity]." Did you catch that? In Christ God has gone to war against the war we started with him. Enmity has been killed by the cross! The result is that "now in Christ Jesus you who once were far off have been brought near by the blood of Christ. For he himself is our peace" (Eph. 2:13–14). Author Jerry Bridges says this about the defeat of hostility with God:

> In our natural state, not one of us would want to be reconciled to God. . . . Even though He is the One offended by our sin, He is the One who makes amends to Himself through the death of Christ. . . . When Jesus satisfied the justice of God and propiti-

ated the wrath of God, He did all that was required to remove the enmity of God toward us. By His death he bridged the vast gulf of divine alienation between us and objectively restored us to a position of friendship and favor with God.[8]

I heard a man talking about reconciliation at a conference recently. He contrasted reconciliation with conflict resolution. Conflict resolution happens when a problem between two persons is resolved through whatever means work. The problem with our enmity with God is that the last thing we want is conflict resolution. The most expedient conflict resolution between us and God is eternal punishment in hell. That would do it.[9] But the boundless love of God did not settle for conflict resolution. Christ has *reconciled* us to God! We become the exact opposite of our state in enmity. By the mercy of God, the covenant promises of God are our promises. If you have been reconciled to God, you are as near as imaginably possible to him. This isn't near as in being "near" to the president when you drive by the White House. This is near as in, now we have unlimited access to God *as Father!* We are related to as favored children of the holy God of the universe. We are *better off* than we were before all this rebellion broke out. Adam's access to God was secured by his obedience to God. Our access is secured by the perfect obedience of the Son.

One of the odd things I noticed in the first few months after my conversion was how I related to the police. For years I had an alienated relationship with the police. I spent considerable time being where the police didn't want me to be, or doing what the police didn't want me to do. Or both at the same time. With conversion, that reality changed. I would be driving down the road and see a squad car and reflexively check around to see if anything in my car was illegal, if I was going the right speed, if the officer in the car was watching me. And then one day I thought, "The police aren't my enemies anymore." I began to gradually lose that aversion to their presence. It got to where I'd wave to them, even go out of my way to respect and appreciate them. I wasn't trained by life to value the police; I had to learn how to do it.

We are not trained by life to want access to God. We are trained by life to run from God, or rail against him. This radical reconciliation opens up an access to something we have long feared. It's understandable that we wouldn't naturally move toward it. That's why we need the Spirit of God as our "access in one Spirit to the Father" (Eph. 2:18) The Spirit not only guarantees our acceptance to God, he also teaches us to desire and enjoy the access we have been given.

A New People of God Has Been Created

Our reconciliation is not simply personal. This troubling problem of Jew and Gentile? Solved. Are Gentiles now Jews? Are Jews now Gentiles? Neither. In Christ the two have been made into one people. This isn't just cleaning up some ethnic divisions. A new people has been created—a people of the reconciliation. All who are reconciled with God become part of this reconciled people. As Paul says it, "We *both* have access in one Spirit to the Father. . . . [We] are fellow citizens with the saints and members of the household of God" (Eph. 2:18–19). This aspect of reconciliation is nothing less than the ultimate key to ending all racial, ethnic, and social strife known to human experience. Pastor/author Thabiti Anyabwile says, "The cross-work of Christ creates a new spiritual ethnicity."[10]

Paul drives this message of reconciliation toward the concept of a new people being built into a living temple, with Jesus Christ as the cornerstone. What Paul is saying is that the reconciliation of God has had as its intended effect not just personal peace with God but the inauguration of a new peace project of God—the church of Jesus Christ. The purpose of Paul's letter to the Ephesians is exactly this: to train this reconciled people to live out the peacemaking purpose of God in the world. He prepares them for the work by calling them to be "eager to maintain the unity of the Spirit in the bond of peace" (Eph. 4:3). He mobilizes them with the "readiness shoes" of the gospel of peace (6:15). At the end of the letter, he reminds them of the Triune God who fuels peace among them and through them: "Peace be to the brothers, and love with faith, from God the Father and the Lord Jesus Christ" (6:23). Reconciliation sweeps each of us into something larger than simply the resolution of our personal God-problems. It takes us into the mission of the gospel!

That's what happened to me in February 1981. I realized that I was ruined for the world that had been my home. I didn't fit its ways anymore. I needed to be where I now belonged. So I found myself wandering into church again. This time it was different. I found myself among my new family. I entered a building made by human hands and found myself in a living temple made by God's hands. I was home.

But something else happened. In coming to terms with my new access to God, my reconciliation with God, my nearness to God, and my connection to God's people, I began to see the world in a different way. I looked around and saw many folks, many of them friends and family, who were still far from God, alienated and destined for the awful conflict resolution of certain judgment and hell. Something in my soul opened my eyes to the reality of people around me who are without God and without hope in the world. That didn't sit right with me. It has never sat right with me. It shouldn't sit right with you, either. Alienation from God is not the way it is supposed to be—it will always be the opposite of shalom. When God returns us to shalom, he enlists us in his shalom work in this alienated world.

We all have a story. What I hope you see in this chapter is that all of our stories ultimately lead to the question of whether we know the Prince of Peace. That is the key to every human story. I encountered the Prince of Peace when I was in a profoundly nonreligious frame of mind. But let me introduce you to a man who knew and sought to live the Christian faith from the get-go. Charles Spurgeon was perhaps the most well-known Christian leader of the nineteenth century. Raised in a profoundly Christian heritage stretching back at least four generations and blessed with an unusual serious desire for God at an early age, it would be hard to imagine a man less likely to be aware of his enmity toward God. But his own words tell us how the gospel invaded below his religious conscience and reconciled his soul to God.

I was once a broken-hearted sinner, cowering down beneath the black cloud of almighty wrath, guilty and self-condemned, and I felt that if I were banished for ever from Jehovah's presence, I could not say a word against the justice of the sentence. When I read in his word, "If we confess our sins, he is faithful and just to forgive us our sins," I went to him. Tremblingly I resolved to test his promise. I acknowledged my transgressions unto the Lord, and he forgave the iniquity of my sin. I am telling no idle tale, for the deep, restful peace which came to my heart in the moment of forgiveness was such that it seemed as if I had begun a new life; as, indeed, I had.

This is how it came about: I heard, one Sabbath day, a poor man speak upon that promise, "Look unto me, and be ye saved, all ye ends of the earth." I could not understand how a mere look to Christ could save me. It seemed too simple an act to effect so great a result; but, as I was ready to try anything, I LOOKED—*I looked to Jesus.*

It was all I did. It was all I could do. I looked unto him who is set forth as a propitiation for sin; and in a moment I saw that I was reconciled to God. I saw that if Jesus suffered in my stead, I could not suffer too; and that if he bore all my sin, I had no more sin to bear. My iniquity must be blotted out if Jesus bore it in my stead, and suffered all its penalty. With that thought there came into my spirit a sweet sense of peace with God through Jesus Christ my Lord. The promise was true, and I found it to be so. It happened some six-and-thirty years ago, but I have never lost the sense of that complete salvation which I then found, nor have I lost that peace which so sweetly dawned upon my spirit. *Since then I have never relied in vain upon a promise of God. I have been placed in positions of great peril, have known great need, have felt sharp pain, and have been weighted with incessant anxieties; but the Lord had been true to every line of his word, and when I have trusted him he has carried me through everything without a failure. I am bound to speak well of him, and I do so.* To THIS I SET MY HAND AND SEAL, without hesitation or reserve.[11]

Religious people, irreligious people, spiritual or secular, we all need peace with God. When we have peace with God, it changes our lives. And we want it to change others as well. That's the radiant beauty of shalom.

Where We're Going from Here

This chapter has touched on some important themes that we'll be developing through the rest of the book as we explore the application of shalom in our lives:

Peace with God gives us enduring confidence that things are the way they are meant to be between us and God.

Peace with God gives us an access to God by the Spirit that enables us to experience true peace in every trial of life.

Peace with God has given us a permanent place in his community of peace that will shape the way we do life in a strife-filled world.

Peace with God creates a passion in our hearts for his mission of peace among people who are still at war with him.

Peace with God provides enduring hope that the peace we experience in part now will be all we know in eternity.

Peace and Stress

HOW'S YOUR PEACE TODAY? In the first three chapters we've identified the problem of peace and God's amazing solution to the problem in Jesus Christ. But how does this play out for us in a stressed-out world? Does the peace we've received in Christ have any impact in our daily grind, or is it simply a religious truth that only works in the confines of religious experience? There is certainly no lack of desire for peace in our hectic world today. We talk about stress a lot. Daily life is lists of things to do and no time to get them done. There exists a common-variety stress that wears us down, blares in our brains, runs us hard in every direction, distracts us to exhaustion, and invades our sleep. We get used to it, but we can't really get away from it. The world of self-help and Eastern spirituality trades on promises of peace in the busy pace of life. Consider the words of one very popular motivational speaker from his best-selling book:

> When you're at peace you radiate a different kind of energy than when you're stressed or depressed. The more peaceful you become, the easier you can deflect the negative energies of those you encounter. This is like having an invisible shield around you that nothing can penetrate unless it's a higher spiritual energy than your shield. A hostile current is greeted with a smile and an inner knowledge that this is not your stuff. A person who attempts to bring you into their misery cannot succeed without your agreement. Your meditation practice keeps you immune. Not only can you deflect the negativity of those around you, but your sense of peace will bring others into harmony with you.[1]

I'm not exactly sure what is being said here, but lots of people seem to think it is good advice. If nothing else, this kind of literature speaks to a common longing for a sense of inner calm and control in the day-to-day troubles of life—a peace vibe, if you will. What should we expect of shalom from God? I believe that the Bible teaches we can have an enduring state of peace with God *and* a true and ongoing experience of peace from God

Jesus himself, the Prince of Peace, promised the experience of peace. In the remarkable conversation around the Last Supper (just before his betrayal and crucifixion) in the Gospel of John, Jesus takes time to reassure his suddenly bewildered disciples. He has just made it clear in word and symbolic action that his time is short and that what is about to happen is not what they have expected. One of them will betray him; another will soon deny him. This three-year adventure in discipleship is about to come to an abrupt end. Jesus will be gone. These men are starting to catch some stress (John 13). Knowing this, Jesus promises them an alternative: "Peace I leave with you; my peace I give to you. Not as the world gives do I give to you. Let not your hearts be troubled, neither let them be afraid" (John 14:27).

Later in the evening (chap. 16) Jesus comes back to this promise of peace. It is necessary, because he has just told his disciples that not only will he go away, but in following him they have signed on for a life of extreme stress. The world will hate them and persecute them. They will be cast out of their community, and even face death at the hands of people who believe persecuting them is doing God's will. Most troubling of all, Jesus has told them that the very next thing they will do, after the Supper, will be to utterly fail the faithfulness test. They will abandon their Lord in his darkest hour and live forever with the memory of that betrayal. So Jesus comes back again to the peace promise: "I have said these things to you, that in me you may have peace. In the world you will have tribulation. But take heart; I have overcome the world" (John 16:33).

The most important thing to understand about these two promises is the source of peace they offer. These promises of peace both come on the heels of the greater promise of the Holy Spirit (John 14:16–26; 15:26–27). Jesus has been the peace of the disciples during his earthly ministry. While he has been with them, they have known shalom. But he is going away. We know (they do not) that he is going to purchase ultimate peace for them on the cross. But he will not leave them bereft of his peace. That peace will come to them through the indwelling of the Holy Spirit. It will be a deeply experiential peace because the Prince of Peace will take up his residence within their hearts in the person and work of the Holy Spirit.

Providing the tangible experience of God's peace in the hearts of God's children is one of the significant activities of the Holy Spirit. Peace is numbered among the fruits of the Spirit in Galatians 5:22—a definable expression of the life of God operating in our souls. Paul also prays for the dynamic peace of the Spirit in the lives of new believers: "May the God of hope fill you with all joy and peace in believing, so that by the power of the Holy Spirit you may abound in hope" (Rom. 15:13). And he prays for peace "at all times in every way" (2 Thess. 3:16) among God's people. Jonathan Edwards sums up this peace-producing work of the Holy Spirit: "The Christian tranquility, rest, and joy of real saints, are not only unspeakable privileges, but they are virtues and graces of God's Spirit."[2]

We should consider the objective peace with God that comes with reconciliation and the experiential peace that comes from the indwelling of the Holy Spirit as different but inseparable manifestations of peace. Any peace a person has apart from reconciliation with God through the atoning death of Jesus Christ is false, damning peace. But because our reconciliation with God brings with it the indwelling presence of God, we should expect and cultivate the peace of God in our souls. I love the way nineteenth-century theologian B. B. Warfield understood this:

> We cannot have peace of heart, until our real and actual separation from God is bridged by the blood of Christ. We cannot have

the breach between God and us healed without a sense of the
new relation of peace stealing into our hearts. And possibly we
cannot do better today than just to realize how interdependent
the two are and how rich the peace is which we obtain in Christ
Jesus. . . . Oh that we may have this peace! Not merely Fundamental peace—though that is the main thing—but Additional peace;
not merely Dormant peace, but Awakened peace—the sense of
being at peace with God.[3]

What a rich description of the shalom of reconciliation. The burden of sin lifted and the gentle filling of the soul by God's Spirit. It
is a reality we are to revel in and cultivate. Let's explore how this
peace is meant to play out in our daily lives.

Unreasonable Peace

The Bible teaches that the peace of a believer is to be an enduring
peace. One of the clearest places this is proclaimed is toward the
end of Paul's letter to the Philippian church. Like the letter to the
Ephesians, this letter does not primarily deal with problems. In
fact, the Philippians held a very dear place in Paul's heart. This
was the first church Paul planted in Europe (Acts 16), and it was a
healthy church that was consistently supporting the church planting mission of its founder. So the tone of the letter is thankful, joyful, and encouraging. It is clear, however, that Paul is not content
to let a healthy church operate on cruise control. He urges them to
walk worthy of the gospel (Philippians 1), follow Christ's example
to lay down their lives in humble service (chap. 2), and follow his
example in pressing on toward the upward call of God in Christ
(chap. 3). Chapter 4 finds Paul addressing some pastoral issues he
knows are occurring in the church. One in particular is an appar-
ent tendency for the people to worry about their circumstances—
in our words, to stress out over things around them. So he writes,

Rejoice in the Lord always; again I will say, rejoice. Let your
reasonableness be known to everyone. The Lord is at hand; do
not be anxious about anything, but in everything by prayer and
supplication with thanksgiving let your requests be made known

to God. And the peace of God, which surpasses all understanding, will guard your hearts and your minds in Christ Jesus.

Finally, brothers, whatever is true, whatever is honorable, whatever is just, whatever is pure, whatever is lovely, whatever is commendable, if there is any excellence, if there is anything worthy of praise, think about these things. What you have learned and received and heard and seen in me—practice these things, and the God of peace will be with you. (Phil. 4:4–9)

The apostle wants peace to flood the Philippian church. God wants this passage to stir peace in our hearts as well. We need peace because the ordinary stresses of life grind on our souls. And we need peace because we venture out into a world of stress every day. Paul's words to the Philippians address both what comes at us and how we need to prepare ourselves to do our business in a stressed-out world.

Peace Guards Us When the Stress of Life Comes against Us

Are you under the duress of stress? You need the straight talk of Scripture. In strong tones Paul first yanks the Philippians' attention off of themselves and their circumstances and calls them to rejoice—to turn their gaze and thoughts upward to the glory of Christ (Phil. 4:4). Why not? Is not the Lord "at hand" (v. 5)? Is he not present and able to handle any and all difficulties they face? Is he not coming back to make right anything that might be wrong? Then go to him with what you need, what you lack (v. 6). Do it confidently, thankfully, specifically, and consistently. And God will give you shalom—something circumstances can never take away.

Verse 7 describes this peace: "And the peace of God, which surpasses all understanding, will guard your hearts and your minds in Christ Jesus." The peace Paul is talking about is experiential calm and rest that is meant to keep us rejoicing regardless of the stressors in our lives. One commentator calls it the "smile of God reflected in the soul of the believer."[4] The peace of God isn't bound by human reasoning. True peace cannot be conjured up by controlling our circumstances or outthinking our stress. Helen

Keller is quoted as saying, "I do not want the peace which passeth understanding, I want the understanding which bringeth peace."[5] The problem with peace that can be obtained by understanding, by figuring things out, is that it is dependent on our ability to figure things out. And that is a very fragile peace. What Paul has in mind is an enduring peace in our hearts that is impervious to the stress and confusion of life. It's a peace more like what commentator Alec Motyer describes:

> What we need today—as at every period of history—is the touch of the supernatural, something that cannot be explained except by saying, "This is the finger of God." This is what is now promised, a peace which passes all understanding standing guard over our hearts.[6]

Paul uses an interesting analogy for how peace will function in our hearts. The concept of "guard" is probably better translated "garrison." It is a military term that has to do with the presence of soldiers strategically placed in a town for its protection and defense. This would have been a very vivid image for the Philippians, since their town was actually resettled after Roman troops conquered it in battle. It was a strategic city for the defense of the empire and its commercial interests in Europe. The people in this church enjoyed firsthand the benefits of the Pax Romana—the Peace of Rome—in protection and security and relative tranquility.

Paul draws on this relative state of guarded peace and applies it spiritually to the hearts of the Philippian believers. The function of a garrison is twofold. It protects the inhabitants from attack from the outside. That's what the peace of God is meant to do for us. Life is ordinary stressors (traffic jams, overwork, money pinches, nitpicky arguments) punctuated by daunting crises, some good (the new baby, moving to a new house, wedding planning) and some traumatic (the death of a loved one, marital separation, significant illness, loss of a job). Scripture promises a peace that allows us to face these high-stress experiences without succumbing to the anxiety that can invasively control our lives. The garrison maintains order within as well. When our hearts are troubled by outward circumstances, when we are tempted to doubt and trust our own understanding, the peace of God brings order that allows us to face the stress of life with abiding joy that is not of our own making.

I had a profound experience of this peace garrison in my life a number of years ago. I had been overseeing a ministry to international students in the city of Philadelphia. In many ways, it was a fulfilling time; I saw the conversion of people from Muslim, Hindu, Shinto, and secular backgrounds. Our team was learning how to build a multi-ethnic community in the city. But like many parachurch ministries, we had limited resources (money). We were always struggling to keep things afloat. I was young and untrained for the ministry and made mistakes that took time and energy to sort out. I was also newly married, and my wife and I were living in a room in a house with fourteen other adults—not the best situation to begin a marriage. I began to burn out, and I struggled with unbelief under the hard work of building the ministry. Around that time my wife and I began to attend a new church plant that offered a weekly men's prayer meeting. One Saturday the church planter said he had a sense that we were to pray for guys there who were frustrated in their present situations. It was not hard for me to raise my hand. As men gathered around me and began to pray, and then to share impressions that they sensed from the Lord for me, a powerful peace came upon me. It was powerful enough where I literally couldn't stand up. So I just lay down on the floor as men prayed for me. It seemed that waves of God's peace were flooding into me, rooting out fatigue and discouragement as they swept through my soul. Eventually the prayer stopped, but I stayed right there on the floor—I didn't want to get up in fear that I'd lose what I was experiencing. I don't know how long I stayed there, although I was aware that people were stepping over and around me to set up for another meeting that was supposed to start after the prayer time. When I finally got up, I felt like things had been put right in my heart. I carried that peace with me back into the stress of ministry. That prayer event occurred over twenty-five years ago. Since that time I have faced much more difficult trials in ministry than anything I faced in that season. But I have never lost the peace that took up garrison in my heart that day. Experiencing the peace that garrisoned in my heart did require something from me. I had to humble myself and make my request known to God. And I have needed to feed that peace as a habit of life over the years. Paul makes it clear that peace comes with the ongoing practice of Godward-looking, Godward-rejoicing, and Godward-praying. Reading God's Word, listening and speaking in prayer, and fortifying my soul with sound theology are the daily troop calls for the peace of God in my life. I'm not talking about some sort of personal work to get close to God—he's already drawn close to us. God isn't pounding on the door of our hearts trying to deliver peace to us. He has come into our hearts by his Holy Spirit. But there are a lot of enemies to peace infiltrating the battle lines of our souls. So we need to diligently engage the peace God has given through regular spiritual devotions.

Chances are this is where you say, "Great, thanks for the failed-devotions guilt trip." Believe me, I am one of the most discipline-challenged people you'll ever know. I have a file drawer filled with well-intentioned but abandoned devotional plans. But I learned something simple that has made a consistent devotional life not only possible, but a reality in my life. Here it is:

The only way we'll ever have consistent, peace-producing spiritual devotions is if we are convinced that God accepts us whether we have them or not!

That's the fact of our reconciliation with God. We come to him already accepted, and the God we come to delights to see us. Now, this doesn't mean that every morning is "power-encounter-with-God" day. No, the devoted life is not spiritual nirvana; it is sowing and reaping. There are days when my devotions are tired, listless, and, frankly, full of hard work. But I've learned that over time, and often in spite of my muddling enthusiasm, God uses the door of devotions to reinforce his peace garrison in my soul.

Besides the fact that a faithful intentional devotional life is a significant means of grace, I'm emphasizing this for a pastoral reason. When I meet with people who are struggling in some profound or ongoing way, I almost never hear them describe a functional devotional life. Maybe the practice had been regular at one time but the stressors of life have undercut it. Or maybe a devotional life never really got off the ground in the first place. What I do know is that nobody wants "let's get your devotional life going" as the first step of pastoral counsel. That doesn't make practical sense as a solution to our problems. We think we need steps and strategies, preferably backed up by Bible promises. That's what works, at least as we understand it. But when we realize that God's peace doesn't require our understanding to take up its post in our hearts, we will tend to move toward the means that he offers—rejoicing, thanking, and praying. The door of devotion. Let's take the advice of Billy Graham, who, looking back on a very busy and fruitful (and no doubt stressful) life at the age of ninety-two, had this to say:

> If I had to do it over again, I'd spend more time in meditation and prayer and just telling the Lord how much I love Him and adore Him and am looking forward to the time we're going to spend together for eternity.[7]

God's Peace Can Go with Us into a Stressed-Out World

God isn't content to wall us up in our garrison of peace, waiting for the enemies of our soul to get bored and walk away. No, to live as God's people we must go out and engage in a world where stress is the way things get done. So the apostle Paul gives us marching orders for how to engage in a world driven by stress without getting caught up in the craziness of it:

> Finally, brothers, whatever is true, whatever is honorable, whatever is just, whatever is pure, whatever is lovely, whatever is commendable, if there is any excellence, if there is anything worthy of praise, think about these things. What you have learned and

received and heard and seen in me—practice these things, and the God of peace will be with you. (Phil 4:8–9)

Everyone feels stress—some thrive on it, others just cope. There is no shortage of stress-relief remedies recommended to survive in our stressful world. Through a quick Internet search, I found a "peace sign stress ball," which is exactly what you'd picture it is. I also discovered a site offering the following advice: "Blue crystals are particularly known for their abilities to reduce the wearer's stress and worry habits, and to increase inner-tranquility and peace." I think I have drain opener at home with blue crystals in it—wonder if that would work? There are breathing techniques, diets, exercises, art therapies—all of which promise to relieve stress. But by far the most commonly suggested stress relief is good, old-fashioned positive thinking—we should treat problems like opportunities, tackling stress one decision at a time.

It might be tempting to see Paul's exhortation in verses 8 and 9 as apostolic self-help. "Think about these things . . . practice these things." But there is a crucial distinction between what Paul offers and just good positive thinking. It is discernment.[8] To be discerning is to be able to judge rightly according to the standards that God uses to judge. Discerning people value what God accepts and reject what God rejects. And they know the difference. "Think about these things" (v. 8) is best understood as "reckon"; in other words, form your perspective around these things. Use them as tools of discernment. The list of things to reckon with that Paul offers is a set of virtues that in some way would be affirmed by any culture. What is different about these virtues is that they have been radically transformed by what these stressed-out Philippian believers have "learned and received and heard and seen" from Paul. And what is that? Read the first three chapters of Philippians: it is the gospel of Jesus Christ.

To live in our contemporary world is to be inescapably assaulted by more information, more choices, more influences, more demands, and more distractions than any people in history.

Even searching out the plethora of remedies for stress is stressful. Everything matters and demands our attention, whether it be a natural disaster far away or a squabble in our local church. There is always someone talking, tweeting, blogging at us—telling us what to be anxious about. Stress is a battle of the mind. We need discernment—a robust gospel paradigm of thinking, a well-tuned spiritual filter, so that the stressors that dominate others' lives don't dominate ours. Let's take a look at what discernment strategies Scripture offers for our peace in this world. Philippians 4:4–6 says that we should think about the following:

"Whatever is true." We are naturally curious folk. We like to figure things out. But the downside is that our earthly peace is dependent on what we know or find out. With the Internet came the ability to get information on almost anything we want. With smart phones we can get anything from stock trends to the latest dish on reality stars while we wait for the traffic light to turn green. But information does not bring peace. Googling a medical diagnosis won't take away our fears of the odd physical symptom we're experiencing. Finding out whatever happened to that old boyfriend through a Google search won't make us happier in our marriage. To battle stress with truth is to reckon that what really matters to us is not information, but what God reveals in his Word. A. W. Tozer tells us what we can expect to get when we allow God's Word to shape our perspective:

> The holy scriptures tell us what we could never learn any other way: They tell us what we are, who we are, how we got here, why we are here, and what we are required to do while we remain here.[9]

Is there really anything else we need to know to be at peace?

"Whatever is honorable." This can also be translated "noble"; in other words, worthy of respect. In our day, honorable doesn't get attention. Let's be honest, it's the sensational stuff that's hard to resist. A political scandal, a lurid crime, the outlandish lifestyle of a celebrity—we're suckers for salacious buzz. We're appalled at

what people are willing to do for fifteen minutes of fame on reality TV or YouTube, but we can't be out-of-the-know when they do it. Media is all too ready to accommodate this mawkish tendency. In a fragmenting media market, the sensational and the crude draw viewers and listeners and website hits. There is no lack of sensational out there—cell phones and paparazzi capture someone in an unguarded moment, websites take it viral, and all mass media needs to do is comment on it. When we eat the cotton candy of cultural sensationalism, we get filled up on the wrong things. We take seriously what should be treated superficially, and therefore we don't train ourselves to think soberly about what matters. When the sensational trains our senses, we are not prepared for the weighty and the truly significant. Discernment trains our minds to focus on what matters, so that we respond rightly to it while letting the trivial and tawdry flow on by.

"*Whatever is just.*" One of the most troubling experiences I have in pastoral ministry is encountering someone who is offended and is demanding justice. Sadly, what I have often found in folks is that they are not really looking for justice. They crave vindication. Let me illustrate. If I am in conflict with someone and believe they have done me wrong, then it is understandable that I would want them to own that wrong and do what is reasonable to make it right. That's justice. But suppose you and I are in conflict and we differ on what really happened. What if I'm not satisfied with your simply acknowledging where you see you're wrong? What if I also insist that you agree that I'm right? That is vindication. Seeking vindication of my perspective, my feelings, or my facts is an unachievable, and more importantly, unrighteous goal. Who, after all, is completely right? There are people, confessing Christians, who get stuck in this hopeless quest for vindication, and they are willing to live contentious, stress-filled, peaceless lives to fight for it. Biblical discernment values justice because it is important to God, not because it is necessary for personal peace. What gets us to peace is not justice, but mercy. Mercy among God's reconciled people always "triumphs over judgment" (James 2:13).

"*Whatever is pure.*" The word *pure* here is often translated "holy." What is being advocated is not what is common, but what is set apart. In a moral sense, purity has to do with motives—why we do things. In our day-to-day lives we don't think about why we do things very much. We're pragmatists; we do what works. But what would life be like if we asked the question "why?" more regularly? Let's get real in the area of self-expression. How should purity affect what we say? How we comment on social media sites or what we say in blogs? Pragmatism doesn't ask why before it does things. It goes to work in the moment. It blurts out that criticism. It tweets and posts and texts whatever it is thinking right now. And then it stresses out because it is always "misunderstood." Purity acknowledges that there is a holy God who sees everything and remembers what he sees. This holy God has called us to a life of purity. Those who value purity are careful with their communication—not because they can't speak their mind, but because they care more about what's on God's heart.

"*Whatever is lovely.*" The 1970s was a hard decade to be a teenager. What we wore as essential clothing had never been in style before and has never come back in style since. It's almost as if some alien race with a perverse sense of humor infected my generation and mind-controlled us into wearing platform shoes, polyester shirts, and wide-cuff plaid slacks. But we all bought into the look. A great unevaluated stressor in our lives is the effect of style and status on how we make our choices. It is often said that our affluent culture has allowed us to elevate wants into needs. We need better TVs, newer cars, bigger houses, faster wireless, and brand-name everything. In my neighborhood the status symbol of choice is dogs, as in purebred, impeccably groomed canines taken out for show walks every day. We have a fat old dog of questionable breeding who is an untrained embarrassment in the neighborhood. My dog doesn't care about her status, or about mine. To the extent that my dog embarrasses me, I have a style and status problem. Style awareness isn't a problem; style enslavement is. When status and style start driving how we spend our money, who we relate to, and how we construct our lives, then the stress of comparison to others will eat us up. Studies show that one of the greatest stressors on young people is the expectations parents place on them to excel, often because the parents' status is determined by their children's achievements. To value the lovely is to discern what is agreeable first of all to God, what matters in his economy, regardless of what it brings or doesn't bring in terms of the world's appreciation. When the world can't determine what we value, life becomes much simpler.

"*Whatever is commendable.*" I was listening to my local sports radio station recently, and the host was interviewing a well-known sports journalist. The reporter was talking about the changes in news coverage with the emergence of the twenty-four-hour news cycle. He said that in the old days a reporter made his reputation by the hard work of researching and breaking a story. But now, with an uncountable number of news outlets groping for content, it is virtually impossible for any reporter to have an absolute claim on breaking a story. So now the goal of reporting is not breaking news, but getting your point of view out in a way that dominates an issue. What results is a loud and loutish news media clamoring to get market share through compellingly packaged news. Complicated issues are reduced to sound bites, and the debates are reduced to good guy/bad guy political posturing. Unfortunately, I think we as Christians are susceptible to this carnival barker treatment of the important issues of the day. We like things simple and straightforward; clarity brings confidence. That's what we like in our politics—the well-packaged, message-honed winner. It seems the biggest question in political elections is not, can this person govern? but, can he or she win? God's people, however, are to be discerning in a way that recognizes the commendable—the enduring and weighty stuff of character—and prizes that, particularly in those to whom leadership is given. History has shown that the greatest leaders are judged not by popularity, but by posterity. In a culture that increasingly values snappy sound bites and snarky commentary over reason and principled discourse, we need biblically robust discernment when we enter the public square.

Commentator G. Walter Hansen sums up what God's people need to take with them into a world driven by stress:

> Paul is calling for followers of Christ to be attentive, reflective, meditative thinkers. Developing a Christian mind and character requires a lifetime of discerning and disciplined thought about all things that are excellent and praiseworthy.[10]

Maybe you can think of some other "excellent and praiseworthy things" that we need to reckon as well. Like all of Paul's lists in the epistles, this set of discernment virtues is representative, not exhaustive. And discernment is not simply limited to spiritual concerns. Discernment is the careful cultivation of a robust, gospel-inflamed biblical worldview that will allow us to engage in the stuff of this world with minimal stress and maximum impact. That's why Paul can say confidently, "The God of peace will be with you." The God of "this peace," the peace that passes understanding, doesn't just send us out into a stressful world. He goes with us into that world to keep our peace and promote his peace through us. The real-time experience of peace comes through the indwelling of God's Spirit and is cultivated by us when we seek to conform our minds and lives to the things that bring glory to the God of peace.

So, how is your peace today?

Peace and Anxiety

Read This First

I'm a guy who needs directions to put something together. Often directions have a section called "Read This First," which basically tells me all the things I should know so I don't misunderstand the real directions. As we head into the next few chapters of this book, we're going to be talking about some heavier situations in which peace is hard to find—fear, grief, and depression. Here's what you need to know before you read these sections so you won't misapply what I'm talking about.

One chapter in a book cannot resolve a serious, life-defining issue. Our problems can be complex, affecting us mentally, emotionally, spiritually, and physically. I am not qualified to evaluate the use of medications in treating the problems we'll be addressing. If you are taking medications for anxiety or depression or other medical disorders, please don't alter anything you are presently doing after reading this material without consulting your doctor. I trust that, rightly administered, they are helping you address issues that underlie your condition. It is these underlying issues that are the focus of the next few chapters.

As a pastor, my orienting view of the human condition is God-centered and biblically derived. This is not the prevailing view of the psychological community historically or in its current practice. Certainly some treatments and therapies can and do positively impact people with life-dominating battles with fear, grief, and depression. These therapies even overlap with basic Christian wisdom and discipleship. What underlies my approach in these next three chapters is not commitment to strategies; it is desperate trust in the transformative power of the gospel.

My Fears at Fifty

I turned fifty a couple of years ago. Fifty is one of those milestone birthdays that just begs for reflection. Half a century of life gone by—there's no fooling yourself on the march of time. About a month before my birthday, I was driving down the highway listening to news radio. A report came on about a bar brawl started by a "fifty-year-old white male." My first thought was, what's an old geezer like that doing picking fights in a bar? My second thought was, "I'm a fifty-year-old white male—that geezer could be me!" Something like a minor panic attack came over me. My mind seized around that thought, and I started getting a little dizzy and felt like I couldn't breathe. I was able to recover by turning the radio to a classic rock station where I was quickly engulfed in the peace of nostalgia.

That little panic episode clued me in to the fact that turning fifty was kind of scary. So I decided to treat myself with a little self-directed immersion therapy. I took time one morning to write up a list of the "Twenty Things I Fear Most at Fifty." In no particular order, here is what I came up with.

Anything bad happening to my wife and children.
Flying over the ocean at night.
The Eagles never winning the Super Bowl in my lifetime.
Doing something that would disqualify me from ministry.
Popping my Achilles tendon.
Divorce.
Having the only music I like on the radio being called "oldies."
Contracting an incurable and ultimately debilitating or life-
    threatening disease.
Terrorist attacks.
Losing all of my retirement savings.
Being falsely accused of a crime.
Being uncool.

Falling away from God.

Being alone when I'm old.

Living in this country as a persecuted Christian.

Being audited by the IRS.

Having a heart attack while shoveling snow.

The experience of rubbing a towel against my teeth.

Hitting a deer with my car.

An unstoppable stink bug infestation.

A quick analysis of my list says a lot. Some fears are serious (falling away from God); some are trivial (being uncool). Some are more statistically likely (hitting a deer) than others (terrorist attacks). Some are very general (what would need to happen to my family for the "bad things" fear to be realized?); others (divorce) are very specific. Some fears I just have to face in order to live life (flying over the ocean); others can be avoided (obey tax laws). And it's not hard to spot some phobic tendencies in a couple of them—I can't rationally explain the towel thing. But there are some common denominators. First, these are not universal fears; they are my fears based on my life. And second, there is not a single one I ultimately can control.

What is your fear list right now? Has it changed over the past ten years? What might it be ten years from now? In this world some fears do come to pass. When our children are young, we fear they'll rebel or make foolish choices in life—and some do. We all fear cancer, and some of us get it. We fear losing our job, then get downsized in a bad economy. The ultimate fear, the fear of all fears, does come true for everyone. We all fear death, and we all will die.

Anxiety and the Human Capacity to Fear

In the last chapter we talked about how shalom makes the crucial difference in a world of stress and anxiety. In this chapter we're going to go deeper, into the heart of anxiety and fear. These are experiences that can dominate our lives and determine our choices, relationships, and even our health and safety. Certainly, where fear reigns there is no peace.

Let's clarify what we're talking about. Fear is a common emotion. From a human standpoint, fear is a physical, mental, and emotional capacity that serves to keep us and others safe from imminent danger. Counselor Elyse Kirkpatrick says, "Physically, fear is a felt reaction to a perceived danger."[1] Suppose you're crossing the street at a busy city intersection and you don't realize that a car is turning right toward you. The horn blares, the tires screech. Without thinking, your body tenses up, your attention rivets to the car, and you jerk back away from the danger. All this is your body doing what it is designed to do when faced with danger. That's fear at work for your good. It's not peaceful, but it is certainly helpful. A person without any fear is truly crazy and probably isn't long for this world.

But there are fears that aren't helpful. Fear is meant to be short-term, spontaneous, and full bodied. If it lingers with us or if it exerts itself apart from imminent physical danger, it can be harmful and debilitating. This is what essentially happens in the experience of anxiety and worry. Counselor Ed Welch draws the distinction between natural fear and anxiety well:

> While "fear" refers to the experience when a car races toward us and we just barely escape, "anxiety" or worry is the lingering sense, after the car has passed, that life is fragile and we are always vulnerable.[2]

I'm going to be using fear, anxiety, and worry somewhat interchangeably; they're related descriptions for the same basic struggle of fear. In one sense fear/worry/anxiety are reality based. There is certainly no lack of things in this world to worry about. But to the extent that we are chronically anxious, we will not live in the good of the peace of God. In fact, anxiety is a peace killer in our souls. Shalom says life is blessing and order; anxiety says life is chaos and impending doom. Peace is enjoyment of the present; anxiety is obsessed with the future, whether that future is decades or just seconds away. Peace quietly trusts God's sovereign control over all things; anxiety lurks in the murkiness of what we don't know or can't predict. Anxiety and fear encamp just beyond our sense of personal security and control and conduct relentless guerilla warfare on our peace.

Diagnosing Fear and Anxiety

Fear and anxiety aren't one-size-fits-all emotions. They vary widely in expression and in intensity. In the world of psychological diagnoses, fears are by far the largest category of disorders. A diagnosable "anxiety disorder" happens when typical worry "becomes an excessive, irrational dread of everyday situations."[3] Generally speaking, people can experience chronic, unprovoked worry; obsessive-compulsive anxieties; panic disorders that seem to take over our bodies; social anxiety disorders that isolate people from others; phobic fears over particular things; and post-traumatic stress disorder (PTSD), where a traumatic experience triggers intense, ongoing fear responses.[4]

Treatment for anxiety disorders targets the thought and behavior patterns that are set in motion when fears manifest. Since these disorders are full-body struggles, affecting hormonal and adrenal function and sleeping and eating patterns, people often take medication to manage the effect of the anxieties so that therapies which address a person's thinking and feeling patterns can be more effective. When dealing with anxiety disorders, we don't always talk about a "cure"; treatment is more about management, progress, and normalization. Probably the vast majority of those reading this book don't struggle with life-controlling fears. But some do, and the fears often manifest without warning.

Pete is a hardworking man who loved supporting his family, listening to music, and watching ice hockey. Until a couple of summers ago. That's when an accidental explosion occurred at work, dousing Pete with flame. At the hospital, Pete was placed in a medically induced coma so that his burn wounds could be addressed. Three days later he awoke a different man. While his burns are healing, miraculously, Pete's mind and soul are still trapped back at the moment of impact. He is being treated for acute anxiety and PTSD. During the first year of his recovery at home, I visited him about once a week. One day I asked him what peace would mean for him right now. Here's what he said:

> Before my accident, peace meant wholeness, completeness, joy, a life of wholeness with God. Now peace just means normal. I just want a normal day where I'm not afraid. And I'm afraid of everything. Peace is not worrying about everything bad that could possibly happen. In normal life you just don't worry about everything that could possibly happen. PTSD has made me hypervigilant. I worry about everything that might happen. For example, I live in fear of crossing a parking lot—what if a car comes and I don't see it? I just bought the strongest cell phone case you can buy because I'm constantly worrying that I'll drop my cell phone and break it. I want to be normal and just fear what everybody else fears. I'm going to miss my son's first hockey game because I'll have a panic attack with all that noise. Medicine is helping me to feel safe in my house, but not outside of it. I feel normal in my safe zone. That's where I have peace.

Talking to Pete reminds me that my own natural "safety zones" are based on a whole lot of assumptions about how things work. Debilitated worriers are like me, except their assumptions about how things work are primarily negative, at least in the area of their fear. Pete's fears limited his world to what he could see and control. That became a safe zone. But that safe zone was threatening to become a prison made of fear. Is there a way out of the bondage of fear to real peace?

The Origin of Fear

The mental health field has made great strides in understanding how fear works and how it can be managed. But the psychological community is unable to determine the cause of life-controlling anxiety. There are theories—evolutionary, genetic, physiological, social, and cognitive sources are all in the mix of possibilities. But like most psychiatric disorders, it's one thing to describe something; it is entirely another to identify its cause. We find a clue to the nature of anxiety in a key word in the description of many of the problems—*disorder*. Fears (as well as other psychiatric maladies) are considered "spectrum disorders"—they exist in every person to some degree. Only when anxiety has life-impairing or life-defining impact is it treated as a disorder. If we say that something is disordered, we assume that there is an order that can get out of whack. That order must have come from somewhere. It is at this point that we move away from the study of "what" to the study of "why." And when we get to the study of why, we enter God's domain.

If this world were a safe place, there would be no fear as we experience fear. Life would be shalom—safe and full and ordered. But this is a disordered world: chaotic, violent, corrupt, and even evil. In an evil world where we are vulnerable to some realistic danger every moment of our lives, everyone can find something to fear all the time. But that's not the way life was originally supposed to be. Fear reflects that we are no longer in Eden. Anxiety, in essence, is the logical experience of disordered shalom.

In truth, there is a fear we're supposed to have. But it is very specific and limited to one object. We are called to fear God. The fear of God, though, is not an anxious, worrying phobia-fear. Jerry Bridges describes the fear of God in wonderfully clear terms:

> There is an infinite gap in worth and dignity between God the Creator and man the creature, even though man has been created in the image of God. The fear of God is a heartfelt recognition of this.[5]

To the person unreconciled to God, that "infinite gap" is the ultimate source of all life-traumatizing fear. Fear of the wrath of God is the base human fear. But to the one who has peace with God, that gap is the place of worship and confidence and peace. The promise of God in the gospel is a fear of God that drives out all other fear. The prophet Jeremiah foretold of this peace-restoring, fear-alleviating reconciliation to God:

Behold, I will gather them from all the countries to which I drove them in my anger and my wrath and in great indignation. I will bring them back to this place, and I will make them dwell in safety. And they shall be my people, and I will be their God. I will give them one heart and one way, that they may *fear* me forever, for their own good and the good of their children after them. I will make with them an everlasting covenant, that I will not turn away from doing good to them. And I will put the *fear* of me in their hearts, that they may not turn from me. I will rejoice in doing them good, and I will plant them in this land in faithfulness, with all my heart and all my soul. (Jer. 32:37–41)

It is the heart of God that his people not live in anxiety and worry. Instead, we can live in the heartfelt joy that the "infinite gap" between us and God has been bridged by the Prince of Peace. That's the good news of the gospel at work. We are meant to live at peace in a world of fear and anxiety. Possibly the clearest help to us in God's Word on a gospel response to anxiety is found in Jesus's teaching in Matthew 6:25–34.[6] Before we look at the text, let me prepare you; Jesus gives some straight talk on worry. So let's prep for the lesson he has for us.

Jesus's teaching on worry in Matthew 6 is in the middle of his Sermon on the Mount, which unfolds from chapters 5 through 7. The Sermon on the Mount is generally considered one of the great ethical teachings in human history. It is filled with clear moral statements and an amazing ethical vision summed up in what is known as the Golden Rule: "Whatever you wish that others would do to you, do also to them" (Matt. 7:12). President Harry Truman once pronounced, "I do not believe there is a problem in this country or the world today which could not be settled if approached through the teaching of the Sermon on the Mount."[7]

The problem with this reverence for the Sermon on the Mount is that it misses the point. Though the Sermon contains profound ethical wisdom, it is not Jesus's great lesson on human morality. It's not really addressed to the world at all. As John Stott explains,

The Sermon on the Mount is the most complete delineation anywhere in the New Testament of the Christian counter-culture.

Here is a Christian value-system, ethical standard, religious devotion, attitude to money, ambition, life-style and network of
relationships—all of which are totally at variance with those of
the non-Christian world. And this Christian counter-culture is
the life of the kingdom of God, a fully human life indeed but lived
out under the divine rule.[8]

If you're looking to live in this world as the world lives, you
won't find much help in what Jesus has to say. As we look at what
Jesus teaches about anxiety, keep this in mind. What makes the
difference in the teaching is the Teacher. You can find peace from
anxiety through what the Teacher says because the Teacher is the
Prince of Peace.

Now let's look at what the Prince of Peace has to say.

Therefore I tell you, do not be anxious about your life, what you
will eat or what you will drink, nor about your body, what you
will put on. Is not life more than food, and the body more than
clothing? Look at the birds of the air: they neither sow nor reap
nor gather into barns, and yet your heavenly Father feeds them.
Are you not of more value than they? And which of you by being
anxious can add a single hour to his span of life? And why are
you anxious about clothing? Consider the lilies of the field, how
they grow: they neither toil nor spin, yet I tell you, even Solomon
in all his glory was not arrayed like one of these. But if God so
clothes the grass of the field, which today is alive and tomorrow
is thrown into the oven, will he not much more clothe you, O you
of little faith? Therefore do not be anxious, saying, "What shall
we eat?" or "What shall we drink?" or "What shall we wear?" For
the Gentiles seek after all these things, and your heavenly Father
knows that you need them all. But seek first the kingdom of God
and his righteousness, and all these things will be added to you.
Therefore do not be anxious about tomorrow, for tomorrow
will be anxious for itself. Sufficient for the day is its own trouble.
(Matt. 6:25–34)

The Prince of Peace Cares for the Anxious Soul

First, don't miss the compassion the Prince of Peace brings to
the anxious soul. In many rebukes and teachings, Jesus confronts

people using words such as "fools," "hypocrites," and the like. But the consistent tone of Scripture to the worrier is mercy and grace.

> When anxiety was great within me,
>> your consolation brought joy to my soul. (Ps. 94:19 NIV)

> Humble yourselves, therefore, under God's mighty hand, that he may lift you up in due time. Cast all your anxiety on him because he cares for you. (1 Pet. 5:6–7 NIV)

And of course the compassion of Jesus is palpable as he addresses the worrying Martha who can't stop serving the Savior for a moment to just be with him (Luke 10:40). Jesus knows the troubles of the people he is addressing. And he knows ours as well. His "do not be anxious" (Matt. 6:25) is a compassionate word. How do you perceive God's view of you in your fears? If you are battling fears and anxiety, know this: the Prince of Peace is never frustrated with you. He has boundless mercy for your fears. The worrier need never worry whether Jesus will have a place in his heart for you.

But Jesus isn't one to offer advice. His words are compassionate, but they are also a command: "Do not be anxious." The word translated as *anxious* is the Greek word *merimno*. It's a word that can have either positive or negative connotations depending on the context of the passage. The basic idea is of something turning us away from something we would ordinarily pursue. In a positive sense, when we *merimno*, we turn our attention from what we are pursuing to something more important. Paul uses it this way, for example, in 1 Corinthians 12:25: "that the members may have the same care [*merinmo*] for one another." So as long as what we turn our attention to is the right thing, and we turn our attention to it in the right way, we are caring rightly. Matthew uses *merinmo* seven times, more than any other New Testament author, but six of those times are right here in chapter 6. And he is not using it positively. The *New International Dictionary of Biblical Theology* gives us an idea of what Jesus is addressing in this command. *Merinmo* in this case is "the natural reaction of man to poverty, hunger and other troubles which befall him in his daily life. Oppressed by the burdens laid upon him, man imagines himself delivered to a fate before which he stands powerless. By his care man tries to protect himself as best he can from what confronts him."[9]

Jesus is exposing the futility of worry. The remedy for anxiety that the Prince of Peace offers begins with seeing it as misplaced *merinmo*. Worry and anxiety, no matter how intense or pathological they become, are the result of focusing on the wrong things at the expense of the right things. I'm not saying that we can simply choose to extract ourselves from debilitating fear. We are complicated people susceptible to entrenched habits of thinking and feeling. But no matter how deep our fear runs, it is essentially misplaced focus. Phobias focus on a particular thing at the expense of anything else. PTSD focuses on bad experiences at the expense of anything else. OCD focuses on patterns at the expense of anything else. Panic attacks focus on fear itself, at the expense of anything else. You and I in our garden-variety anxieties are distracted by the wrong cares, at the expense of the right cares. The Prince of Peace tells us to consider where we are placing our care.

The Prince of Peace Counsels the Anxious Soul

> Look at the birds of the air: they neither sow nor reap nor gather into barns, and yet your heavenly Father feeds them. Are you not of more value than they? And which of you by being anxious can add a single hour to his span of life? And why are you anxious about clothing? Consider the lilies of the field, how they grow: they neither toil nor spin, yet I tell you, even Solomon in all his glory was not arrayed like one of these. But if God so clothes the grass of the field, which today is alive and tomorrow is thrown into the oven, will he not much more clothe you, O you of little faith? Therefore do not be anxious, saying, "What shall we eat?" or "What shall we drink?" or "What shall we wear?" For the Gentiles seek after all these things, and your heavenly Father knows that you need them all. (Matt. 6:26–32)

The Prince of Peace now gets to the nub of the problem. Anxiety ignores the love and provision of the Father on our behalf.

Counselor David Powlison makes an interesting point about the birds of the air and the flowers of the field. These aren't chirping, yellow parakeets and vibrant orchids that Jesus is talking about. Jesus is preaching on a dry rocky mountain in a very inhospitable place for delicate flora and fauna. The birds are probably crows (or think city pigeons or pestering seagulls), and the flowers are weeds with buds on them.[10] What they have in common is that both are subsistence creatures—they have no guaranteed habitat or food source. The birds and the flowers flourish in spite of the environment. The point Jesus seems to be making is that circumstances don't determine our ability to flourish. Shalom—abundance and security regardless of circumstances—is a gift that comes from the Father to us because of our reconciled relationship to him. Jesus's words do imply the promise of material provision, but they are not limited to what we eat, drink, and wear. There is far more needed for life than that. And that's what we should care about most.

In verse 30 the Prince of Peace diagnoses the heart problem under anxiety. He chides these worriers for their "little faith." This is a kind way to say a strong thing. In all of the other places where Jesus addresses "little faith" in Matthew's Gospel, the disciples have actively denied that God is with them: the calming of the waves, walking on water, feeding the multitudes. In these situations the disciples have to practically stumble over Jesus to get to fear. And he has to perform a miracle to remind them why fear is absurd. "Little faith" is only used in relation to the disciples. It is not disbelief. It is the lack of faith where faith should be expected. John Piper says, "The root cause of anxiety is a failure to trust all that God has promised to be for us in Jesus."[11]

Lurking in the shadows of anxiety and little faith is the soul-devouring sin of unbelief. In my counseling experience over the years, I've found that people are far too tolerant of unbelief in their lives. They tend to treat it as a mild spiritual cough that you can get used to rather than the deadly "wound of secret godlessness"[12] that infects any sense of peace we have in life. Puritan pastor Thomas Watson warns:

Unbelief is worse than any other sin, because it brings God into suspicion with the creature. It robs him of the richest jewel in his crown, which is his truth: "He that believeth not God hath made him a liar." (1 John 5:10)[13]

Statements like "I'm not really ready to trust God for that" and "That's fine for you, but I'm not sure I believe that for me" aren't just statements of how we feel; they are direct denials of the very truth that makes for peace in our lives. The remedy for unbelief is repentance—turning away from any thinking that denies or diminishes the truth of God's word, and then making small decisions to believe God at his word. A woman who battles fears once handed me a jar of tiny little specks. She said, "Here, these are mustard seeds. When I'm battling fear, I take one of these out and hold it." I opened the jar and tried to put one in my hand. A little pile poured out, and half of those rolled out of my hand and were lost in the pile of the carpet. I was finally able to isolate one in my hand. It was so small, I couldn't even feel it in my palm. Interestingly, later in Matthew Jesus chastises his disciples for "little faith." He then tells them that what is needed to move mountains is faith the size of a mustard seed—a faith you couldn't even feel if you could hold it in your hand (Matt. 17:19–20). Friend, if you battle fear and anxiety, fear unbelief most of all. Unbelief can hold a mustard seed of faith in its hand and deny it exists because it can't be felt. Faith is believing that the Prince of Peace understands our need, and that his Father (and ours) knows how to meet it.

The Prince of Peace Offers the Anxious Soul a Way Out of Fear

But seek first the kingdom of God and his righteousness, and all these things will be added to you.
Therefore do not be anxious about tomorrow, for tomorrow will be anxious for itself. Sufficient for the day is its own trouble. (Matt. 6:33–34)

Esteemed Harvard psychologist Richard McNally says something we should take to heart: "The disorder is always worse than the thing you fear."[14] In other words, what we do with our fears—how they shape us, how we learn to cope with them, can define us far more than whatever we fear. That is the awful paradox of anxiety. The Prince of Peace entered a world of sin-sick and fear-ravaged souls whose coping strategies led them everywhere but to the God who held the cure. So he came to bring that cure in the form of a new kingdom, a kingdom ruled by shalom. To seek first the kingdom isn't some mystical withdrawal from the world, or a denial of the practical needs of life to seek spiritual tranquility. It is receiving the remedy that God has sent our way. I love the detail Jesus adds to his anxiety teaching as recorded in Luke: "Fear not, little flock, for it is your Father's good pleasure to give you the kingdom" (Luke 12:32).

The Father delighted to send the Son to bring the kingdom of shalom to us. We seek it by receiving it and living as if it is real and enduring. Anxiety has no property rights in the kingdom of shalom. The Prince of Peace has outlawed it in his realm. How do we live in the good of this kingdom? We begin by letting tomorrow's troubles worry about themselves. Kingdom peace acts on what faith calls us to act on, and releases what faith requires us to release. The adventure of faith is learning how to do this day by day.

What are some ways you can practically express faith to battle your anxiety? Here is a list that can position you to better battle the disorder of anxiety with the measure of faith God has given.

1. Don't treat chronic or debilitating fear simply as emotional or spiritual weakness. Recognize that our whole being is wrapped up in fear and needs to be considered. Consult with your physician about the possibility of any physiological factors that could contribute to anxiety tendencies. For example, sleeplessness is increasingly seen as a significant contributor to anxiety disorders. When we don't sleep well, we worry, and when we are awake, we function with inhibited capacity to think clearly and biblically about what tempts us to anxiety.

2. Open up the area of fear with a trusted and biblically sound friend, pastor, or counselor who can help you begin to see

tendencies or patterns in your fears and give insight into how to address them. Often what seems like a chaotic emotional mess to us is really an entrenched pattern of thinking and doing that others see rather clearly.

3. Learn the basics of the fear tendencies you have. Anxiety thrives on the way we fill in the unknowns with what seems true or feels right. The more we demystify anxieties, the more we can control them. I had a fear of heights growing up that was conquered only when I took a job painting houses and had to climb ladders. Taking steps to confront a specific fear isn't a cure, but it is pretty certain you won't overcome a fear by avoiding it altogether.

4. Look at what you are emotionally sensitive to. If your daily intake of news or media is saturated with violence or unsettling imagery, consider whether you may be feeding the fear. Some people are more sensitive to strong or disturbing content than others. I haven't watched a horror movie in years because the imagery seems to stick in my mind far too long. What others are fine with may not be fine with you.

5. If you struggle with intense physical manifestations of fear, learning ways to "ride it out" through breathing, movement, talking, praying, etc., can help you get on top of the fear—to bring it under relative control so you handle it wisely. Panic attacks are fears of fear itself. Have a plan to execute that will help calm your soul if you are faced with them.

6. Don't let fear isolate you. Be involved with other people and share their suffering and yours. We all have problems; fear just might be yours. But that doesn't mean you can't contribute to the spiritual growth of your friends as you walk out the fight with fear in fellowship. Don't keep all that good sanctification to yourself.

Finally, begin and end your days with the comfort of the gospel. Because the Prince of Peace has come to fearful people, has died to remove the ultimate fear of judgment, and has given them peace with God through his atoning blood, fear need not disorder your life. No matter what anxieties lurk in your tomorrow, the words of old Puritan John Flavel are true today: "Everything is well, and shall be well, when all is well between us and God."[15]

Peace and Grief

I HAVE A HOBBY some people find odd. I call it "grave searching." Over the years I've found it fascinating to search out the final resting places of historic people. When I know I'm going to be in a new place, I'll research and find out what notable figures are buried there. Presidents, theologians, soldiers, and sports heroes are all subjects of my quest. Buffalo Bill in Denver? Been there. George Whitefield in Massachusetts? Seen him. Michelangelo in Florence? I made the pilgrimage. Why grave searching? Maybe because I'm a history guy, and this is tangible history. Or maybe because pondering the inevitable earthly end of the great and the small helps me use my short time here to greater purpose. Ok, maybe that's a reach. But I do know the hobby has led me to some unexpected encounters with real live people along the way. Some have touched my soul.

One happened earlier this year. I was with my friends David and Zac in Brooklyn, exploring Green-Wood Cemetery, a beautiful historic cemetery on a hill with a stunning view across the East River toward Manhattan. One of the graves we were researching was that of Jean-Michel Basquiat. Basquiat was a prominent artist in the 1980s whose life tragically ended with a drug overdose at the age of 27. I've always found Basquiat's work provocative and arresting, so I wanted to see where he was buried. Though we had a map from the cemetery office that showed the approximate location of Basquiat's headstone, when we got to the section we couldn't find his plot. After about fifteen minutes of wandering around among the graves, we saw a small elderly gentleman approaching us. He said, "You looking for that artist? I'll show you where he is. He's buried behind my daughter."

The little stooped-shouldered man walked us down a row of low symmetrical headstones, literally back-to-back with each other. "Here's my daughter. He's on the other side." Then he set to the sad dignity of clearing away leaves and weeds from his daughter's stone. We stood there for a few minutes, silent, looking down at the grave of a marvelously gifted man whose life was cut short in its prime. A few feet away a grieving father faithfully tended the final resting place of a young woman whose gifts and story are unknown to the world.

As we turned to leave, I wondered if this wasn't an opportunity to offer him some kind of consolation. As I thanked him for helping us, I said, "Sir what you're doing speaks deeply to me—thank you . . ." But before I could finish, he gently held up his hand; the tears in his eyes told me there was a bridge of connection he didn't want to cross. "You never want to do what I'm having to do."

As I think about my own life, I desperately want to believe that I really *won't* have to do what he was doing. But I can't. Because in my own way and my own time, I will have to do what he had learned to do in his own quiet way. I will have to grieve. In truth, I already have tasted the bitterness of grief in my life—the loss of family and friends through death. You have, too. As long as death is the universal human experience, we will all be caught in the inevitable wake that it leaves behind. We will all grieve.

The War on Peace

Grief is the internal experience of human loss. It is often distinguished from bereavement, which is the actual loss of something or someone. Bereavement is a fact; grief is the experience of that fact. While we most often associate grief with death, in his book *A Grief Sanctified: Through Sorrow to Eternal Hope*, J. I. Packer expands the experience of grief into many areas of human loss.

Grief is the inward desolation that follows the losing of something or someone we love—a child, a relative, an actual or anticipated life partner, a pet, a job, one's home, one's hopes, one's health, or whatever.[1]

It is the "whatever" that makes the onset and experience of grief seem so random. I remember when we moved from our first house to the house we live in now. The facts were that we were moving to a nicer home in a better area, closer to friends and fellowship. The day we closed on the sale, I took one last walk through the now empty house—the house where all my kids had been born and where we had learned how to be a family. I couldn't stop crying. I wasn't losing my children—they were moving with me—but I was losing part of my life just the same. It was a part I'd never get back, and I was grieving its loss. To this day when I drive by there I tear up. Life is filled with many small and monumental "grievances." These are but a reflection of the great and irreclaimable loss we know as death. As we turn our attention to how peace addresses grief, I'm going to focus on the grief of death bereavement. If you are experiencing another grief—the loss of a child to marriage, the pain of separation or divorce, the end of your career—whatever that grief may be, my hope is that your grief will not be trivialized as I give attention to the universal experience of grieving the loss of a loved one to the end of life.

If, as some have said, death is the enemy of peace, then grief is the war death wages on peace among those left behind. In chapter 2 we talked about shalom as it is experienced in harmony, order, and fullness. How does the war of grief do damage to shalom in our lives?

Grief Wages War on Harmony

Death forcibly ends the relationship between us and the person we lose, but grief can have ongoing destructive effects on those who are left behind. A family may come together to weather a funeral but erupt in bitterness and division over unresolved conflicts or the messy matters of a family estate. When someone loses a spouse, the "couple" relationships that were so normal stop working. What had symmetry is now always out of whack—the widowed live as an extra wheel in relationships where they used to have equal standing. Every grieving person has had the sadly awkward experience of encountering people who just don't know what to say. C. S. Lewis, in *A Grief Observed*, his raw journal on his own grief at losing his wife to cancer, puts us there in that strange disharmony of personal interaction.

> An odd byproduct of my loss is that I'm aware of being an embarrassment to everyone I meet. At work, at the club, in the street, I see people, as they approach me, trying to make up their minds whether they'll "say something about it" or not. I hate it if they do, and if they don't.[2]

On a plane flight recently I was working on material for this book. I struck up a conversation with a woman named Bar Scott in the seat next to me. When I told Bar I was working on a book, she said, "I'm a writer too." I asked her what she had done, and she told me that she had written a memoir on the death of her only son, Forrest, who had contracted a rare form of cancer and died after "1,266 days of joy" on earth. It was evident from what she said that she had done well with her grief and was very spiritually minded, though she did not claim to be a Christian. In our conversation I was able to talk about the peace of Christ that I was writing about in my book. When I got to Denver, I downloaded her book *The Present Giver* and read it on the return flight. It was a very honest and moving account of living through what most parents would consider their worst nightmare. What I appreciated about Bar's work was how she captured the hidden moments of anguish in grief. She wrote about how hard it was to even have casual conversation after Forrest died.

> Whenever someone asks me if I have children, I have a choice to make: tell them the truth or lie. If the situation allows for

me to be honest, I tell the truth; if the truth will not be helpful in any way, I lie. A few months ago, I got my hair cut in a new salon. When my head was dangling over the sink behind me to be shampooed, the hairdresser said, "So, do you have any children?" I didn't know this woman, but my sense was that she was going to be a talkative stylist, so I paused to consider my response. After a beat or two, I said, "No, I don't." She obviously assumed she was in the clear, so with relief she said, "Oh you're so lucky! I love my daughter more than anything, but she's so damn much work. I don't even have a life anymore." As it happened I was missing Forrest a lot that day, so I let the tears roll down the side of my face and pretended there was soap in my eyes. I let her vent her frustration though. My darker side was tempted to follow up with the truth later on, but I never did.[3]

Bar Scott graciously handled a situation that every grieving person can sadly identify with. Even the simplest human encounters can become awkward discords. When the war with grief comes, harmony with others cannot escape collateral damage.

Grief Wages War on Order

From the moment we experience loss, there is a massive disruption in the rhythms of life. Everything that was routine is up for grabs. New, unpleasant duties are thrust upon us—purchasing death certificates, changing policies, doing something with the belongings of the deceased. Whole areas of life suddenly become shrines—rooms in the house, former special places—that are now haunted by painful memory. And all plans for the future are put on indefinite hold. One of the unanticipated traumas of grief is what happens after the immediate ceremonial activity ends. As hard as funerals and memorial services are, they do have one great benefit. They give focus; they allow us to engage in activities that seem consistent with our loss. But after the service, everyone else moves back into familiar life patterns, while the grieving move . . . into, well, we're not quite sure. It's an unsettling experience to be staring at a disrupted future. Lewis captured this intimidating orderlessness well.

Grief still feels like fear. Perhaps, more strictly, like suspense. Or like waiting; just hanging about waiting for something to happen. It gives life a permanently provisional feeling. It doesn't seem worth starting anything. I can't settle down. I yawn, I fidget, I smoke too much. Up till this I always had too little time. Now there is nothing but time. Almost pure time, empty successiveness.[4]

The "empty successiveness" of grief can overrun order in every part of life.

Grief Wages War on Fullness

One of the most common words used to describe grief is "void." In normal experience, relationships can clutter our lives. Time demands, inconvenient and difficult conversations, conflicts and misunderstandings, and emotional expectations can cause us to long for a little more time to ourselves. Then death or separation removes a person from our lives, and we realize how much of who we are disappears with the loss. We are not full in ourselves; we discover how our lives are compiled in many ways from the relational strands that are woven into them. Yale philosophy professor Nicholas Wolterstorff lost his twenty-five-year-old son to a hiking accident. In his book devoted to that loss, *Lament for a Son*, Wolterstorff poignantly describes the inescapable sense of emptiness that grief brought to his life.

It's the neverness that is so painful. Never again to be here with us—never to sit with us at table, never to travel with us, never to laugh with us, never to cry with us, never to embrace us as he leaves for school, never to see his brothers and sisters marry. All the rest of our lives we must live without him. Only our death can stop the pain of his death. . . . There's a hole in the world now. In the place where he was, there's now just nothing. A center, like no other, of memory and hope and knowledge and affection which once inhabited this earth is gone. Only a gap remains. A perspective on this world unique in this world which once moved about within this world has been rubbed out. Only a void is left. There's nobody now who saw just what he saw, knows what he knew, remembers what he remembered, loves what he loved. A person, an irreplaceable person, is gone. Never again will anyone apprehend the world quite the way he did. Never again will anyone inhabit the world the way he did. Questions I have can never now get answers. The world is now emptier. My son is gone. Only a hole remains, a void, a gap, never to be filled.[5]

If you have experienced a life-altering loss in the death of a loved one, or a death of any kind, the fight for peace can be the fight for life. Is there hope for peace?

Unbearable Pain Meets Unreasonable Peace

Giving advice to those who mourn is a treacherous thing. There are a lot of good things that grieving people probably need to know, but may not be ready to hear. The wrong person bringing something at the wrong time will make even good counsel a bad experience. Often the hardest words to hear are religious words. That was the experience of Job, whose "counselors" were well intended but pastorally deaf. If you are in mourning right now, I want to speak to you with the rest of this chapter. Not everything I have to say may fit where you at this moment, and that's OK. But I have three simple points that I hope lodge somewhere in your heart and mind, and at the proper time and in the proper way, give light in dark times. My three points are:

> Grief has a divine Comforter.
> Grief has a divine remedy.
> Grief has a divine end.

Grief Has a Divine Comforter

In the year 381, Bishop Gregory of Nyssa, one of the "Cappadocian Fathers" in church history, preached the funeral sermon of his friend and fellow bishop, Meletius. As he spoke, Gregory opened a window into the travails of his own soul: "How can I lift up the eyes of my soul, veiled as I am with this darkness of misfortune? Who will pierce for me this deep dark cloud of grief, and light up again, as out of a clear sky, the bright ray of peace?"[6]

In his anguished words Gregory profoundly places the focus where it should be. The problem of grief is really the problem of death (Gen. 2:15–17). And the problem of death lies at the feet of God. It is God who created a world with the possibility of death. When an infinite being creates, he cannot create other infinity. Everything he creates has finiteness; it has boundaries. And when the created seeks to live as if it were self-existent, it loses the very life it has been given. This is death in its cosmic sense. In chapter 2 we covered the primal creation and fall of mankind. As we saw, death is an inevitable experience of the creature rebelling against the limits of its existence—its dependence on the Creator for life and meaning. Shalom was the order that God set in creation; mankind rebelled against that order and, in doing so, cast off shalom and embraced in consequence the enemy of shalom—death. And because death is the enemy of shalom, a shalom-loving God must hate death.

Let's be careful here. To say that God hates death seems to fly in the face of the abundance of death that occurs in relation to God, particularly in the Old Testament. Wherever God is, death seems to be close by. But we must separate the necessity of judgment for sin, which underlies all of God's death activity in the Bible, with the human experience of death. God judges and punishes according to his holy character and word, but he didn't create this world or populate it with the ultimate goal of judgment. Judgment of sin is a necessary action for God to exercise because he is Ultimate Judge of wrong, and wrong must ultimately be done away with. But God takes no enjoyment in death. Death is unclean to God (Num. 9:1–10). God receives no worship in death (Pss. 6:5; 30:9); he is a compassionate deliverer from death for many (Psalms 107; 116); and even if death comes, it has precious weight to God (Ps. 116:15). Paradoxically, fearing God is actually a life-affirming/death-opposing stand for someone to take (Prov. 14:27). We know most assuredly God's stance on death because he sent his own beloved Son into its very jaws, so that the defeat of death would be accomplished and we would find life. This defeat was accomplished in the resurrection (1 Cor. 15:12–22). God's triumph over death is trumpeted by the apostle Peter: "Blessed be the God and Father of our Lord Jesus Christ! According to his great mercy, he has caused us to be born again to a living hope through the resurrection of Jesus Christ from the dead" (1 Pet. 1:3).

Resurrection is the unique Christian answer to death. But what about grief? How do we cope with death that leaves the living behind? The Bible teaches something remarkable. Death in this world is not final. Death is not the end of cosmic existence— that would be annihilation. Death is the end of existence on this earth, in anticipation of an eternal life in another state. This is important theologically and emotionally. Theologically it means that persons have a limited time here to prepare for eternity. Those who don't prepare well face a future of perpetual eternal judgment—what is frighteningly called the "second death" (Rev. 20:14; 21:8). In a sense, grief happens because time is short. Emotionally, for us who grieve, it is important to embrace the literal physicality of death. A person who was a living, breathing image bearer of God (for that is what we all are) becomes "a body," a thing to be handled in culturally and legally appropriate ways. When we see a loved one at a viewing, we never equate the body in a casket with the person who held our hand just a few days before. What is left after the "disposition of the body" are memories and effects but no longer a person in this world. Whatever form grief takes in our experience, it must confront the physicality of death. We must initially engage the enemy Death on its turf. The rituals of funeral, memorial, and bereavement help us to enter the travail of grief with something to ground us in reality. Death happens, therefore grief happens.

This brings us back to Gregory's question: "Who will pierce for me this deep dark cloud of grief, and light up again, as out of a clear sky, the bright ray of peace?" The answer is the Prince of Peace. The Prince of Peace is "the resurrection and the life" (John 11:25), the ultimate defeater of death itself (1 Cor. 15:20–26). For those who believe in him he gives eternal life, which is life in relationship with God in God's kingdom.[7] But what about grief? Grieving the loss of a loved one is not the same as fearing our own death. Jesus may be the conqueror of death, but where is he in grief? Friend, know this. One of the most important ministries the Prince of Peace came to do is to bring comfort to those who grieve. Consider his foundational kingdom teaching in the Beatitudes: "Blessed are those who mourn, for they shall be comforted" (Matt. 5:4).[8] Jesus doesn't pick this promise out of a box. It draws its weight from the songs of the Suffering Servant/Prince of Peace in Isaiah, whom we encountered in chapter 2. In Isaiah 60–61 we see just how important it is to the Prince of Peace to come alongside those who grieve. Please take time to read these chapters, particularly 60:17–61:3, where we discover that the Prince of Peace will settle peace over us (60:17). He will himself be the light in our darkness (60:19). He will bring seasons of mourning to an end (60:20). He will bind up our broken hearts (61:1). He will comfort those who are now grieving (61:2). This Prince of Peace will give those who grieve "a beautiful headdress instead of ashes, the oil of gladness instead of mourning, the garment of praise instead of a faint spirit; that they may be called oaks of righteousness, the planting of the LORD, that he may be glorified" (61:3).

As if there were any doubt that Jesus came looking for grieving people, note that it is this passage he chooses as his first teaching in the synagogue, according to Luke, closing his comments with, "Today this Scripture has been fulfilled in your hearing" (Luke 4:21). And his ministry matches his words. In the three places in the Gospels where Jesus raises the dead (the widow and her son [Luke 7:11–17]; Jairus's daughter [Luke 8:40–56]; and the raising of Lazarus [John 11:1–46]) the Gospel writers take pains to show the compassionate heart of Jesus for those who are grieving. The fact that he will shortly and miraculously remove the cause of their grief does not render him compassionless toward it. Before he raises the dead, he weeps with the living! That's how much grief matters to him. If you are grieving now, know that the Savior who raises from the dead is the "man of sorrows, and acquainted with grief; . . . Surely he has borne our griefs and carried our sorrows" (Isa. 53:3–4).

Grief Has a Divine Remedy

The Prince of Peace as our Divine Grief-bearer means that we have something those who don't know him don't have. We have hope (1 Thess. 4:13). Now, truth be told, no one who grieves ever feels like hope is enough. Wolterstorff, a sound Christian theologian as well as philosopher, found hope frustrating.

> Elements of the Gospel which I had always thought would console me did not. They did something else, something important, but not that. It did not console me to be reminded of the hope of the resurrection. If I had forgotten that hope, then it would indeed have brought light into my life to be reminded of it. But I did not think of death as a bottomless pit. I did not grieve as one who has no hope. Yet Eric is gone; *here and now* he is gone, *now* I cannot talk with him, *now* I cannot see him, *now* I cannot hug him, *now* I cannot hear of his plans for the future. That is my sorrow. A friend said, "Remember, he's in good hands." I was deeply moved. But that reality does not put Eric back in my hands *now*. That's my grief. For that grief, what consolation can there be other than having him back?[9]

This is an important point. I believe there is a tendency to "oversell" hope in grief—as if by just talking about hope we can end grief. My friend John, who lost his wife unexpectedly about a year and a half ago, told me recently that grief to him is "heart sickness." Believing the right things keeps him going, but it doesn't keep his heart from being sick. Hope cannot be a cure for grief, but it is a truly effective remedy. The Latin root of the word *remedy* is *remedium*, meaning that which heals again (and again). Metaphorically speaking, hope is meant to function like a remedy, salving the pangs of grief over time. Deep down we know that grief is not a pure emotion. It is contaminated with fear and doubt and anger and self—festering grief can ruin a soul. Hope draws the poison of self and despair out of grief, and replaces it with peace. Hope is the grace of God at work in the grieving heart to move it toward trust and faith. It is comfort that brings strength. "Now may our Lord Jesus Christ himself, and God our Father, who loved us and gave us eternal comfort and good hope through grace, comfort your hearts and establish them in every good work and word" (2 Thess. 2:16–17).

What hope does is make it possible for a grieving person to find peace when there is no earthly reason to be at peace. My friends Jeff and Debbie lived out remarkable hope in the grief over the death of their infant daughter Destiny. Destiny had a rare birth defect that made it unlikely she would survive childbirth. But she did, though her massive physical birth defects left no prognosis of survival. When they dedicated Destiny at church in the first few weeks of her life, Debbie shared her perspective to the people. Listen to the hope.

> It seems Destiny is here just for us. God has packaged up a little life for us to experience more of him. To dedicate Destiny today is special because, despite her condition, we know that before the creation of time, God wanted Destiny to be in our family. We want to embrace what he has for us through her life. We want to celebrate the fact that God is good all of the time, that his ways are perfect even though they don't always look that way in the moment. It's an opportunity to trust God in a way that we've never had to before and to honor him as we walk through something that he has carefully and lovingly chosen to accomplish his good purposes for our whole family.

A few weeks later Destiny's brief life on earth did come to an end. And Debbie shared once again at the memorial service.

> My dear, sweet Destiny died two days ago. It's amazing how you could love someone who did so little so much. She was mine, especially designed by God for me for a time such as this, and I loved her. I cried many nights since she was born—saddened by what her future held and fearful of when her last day would come. I would have never chosen this trial. The pain of losing

a child is at times unbearable. Yet, by God's grace, I was able to press into God and try to see what purpose he had in bringing Destiny into my life—because I have no doubt that God doesn't allow anything without a specific purpose. He had everything calculated down to the minutest detail, including the perfect number of her days to accomplish the purpose that he had in mind for us. He knew the exact amount of pain and emotional energy that I could handle to keep me pressing into him—that it wouldn't be too much that I would grow weary or bitter. I always knew, and still continue to rest on the fact, that he is good all of the time. Not only is he good—but all things that he allows into our lives are for our good.

It all hurts right now in an emotional way—like surgery on our souls. God doesn't allow pain for the sake of pain—but has a plan even for the pain that seems unnecessary. We just can't see the work that he is inevitably doing beneath the surface. May we not miss what he intends!

Jeff and Debbie grieved, and they still carry Destiny in their hearts several years later. But hope has brought comfort to them, and they have not missed what he intended. They have peace.

Grief Has a Divine End

While hope can allow us to experience the peace of God in our grief, it cannot end grief. Tears flow because our lives are gashed by the loss of people and things we love. We long for grief to stop, but that can only happen if the loss never happened in the first place. Author and counselor Paul Tripp speaks to the deep longing for the end of grief.

> Death is the living enemy of everything that is good and beautiful about life as God planned it. Death should make you morally sad and righteously mad. Death is a cruel indicator that the world is broken and not functioning according to God's original design. In his plan, life was to give way to life, giving way to life on into eternity. It is biblical to treat death as the sad, unnatural thing that it actually is. God encourages you to mourn. Death was simply not meant to be. When you recognize this, you will hunger for the complete restoration of all things. You will long to live

with our Lord in a place where the last enemy—death—has been
defeated.[10]

So where does the lament of grief end? Does it end? The Bible
answers the question graphically, emphatically—gloriously! In the
last few chapters of the book of Revelation, the last book of the
Bible, we learn that death itself will end. It will be, as the apostle
Paul declares, "swallowed up in victory" (1 Cor. 15:54). This is the
fruit of the resurrection of Jesus Christ. But it's not the end of the
story. After death meets its untimely end, there is still the problem
of grief—the scar in our lives due to loss—to be dealt with. So we
read in John's vision:

> Then I saw a new heaven and a new earth, for the first heaven
> and the first earth had passed away, and the sea was no more. And
> I saw the holy city, new Jerusalem, coming down out of heaven
> from God, prepared as a bride adorned for her husband. And I
> heard a loud voice from the throne saying, "Behold, the dwelling
> place of God is with man. He will dwell with them, and they will
> be his people, and God himself will be with them as their God.
> He will wipe away every tear from their eyes, and death shall be
> no more, neither shall there be mourning, nor crying, nor pain
> anymore, for the former things have passed away."
> And he who was seated on the throne said, "Behold, I am
> making all things new." (Rev. 21:1–5)

The answer to grief isn't simply the eradication of death. It
is the personal care and comfort of God. He will wipe away your
tears—your grief will be a former thing. Grief will pass away, never
to return. If death is swallowed up in victory, grief will be swallowed up by peace. How do we know? Death meets its end in the
judgment of God (Rev. 20:14). Where does grief meet its final end?
The New Jerusalem. The city of eternal peace. Where the Prince of
Peace makes all things new.

If you grieve, this glimpse of the city of eternal peace was
meant for you to ponder, to tuck away in your heart. It is coming
and you can look forward to it. And the Prince of Peace will com-

fort you with his peace. But there is also something important for you to do with the time you have now. You can help others. You can comfort others with the comfort you receive from God (2 Cor. 1:2–4). That word *comfort* that Paul uses in 2 Corinthians is robust. To comfort is to come alongside others and give them what they need to meet the challenges they face. Maybe it's sympathy. Maybe it's straight talk. Maybe it is just sitting with someone in mourning and letting him cry without saying a thing. Author Nancy Guthrie, who writes from grief in her life for the comfort of others, talks about the effect of quiet, close comfort in mourning.

> It is those who shed their tears with me that show me we are not alone. It often feels like we are carrying this enormous load of sorrow, and when others shed their tears with me, it is like they are taking a bucket full of sadness and carrying it for me. It is, perhaps, the most meaningful thing anyone can do for me.[11]

People acquainted with grief and remedied by hope are meant to make a huge difference in this world. And not just to the grieving world. I meet with John, the friend I mentioned earlier, for breakfast every month or so and we talk about life, and loss. He is still hurting, still trying to figure out a life he didn't plan to live. As he says, "I don't feel like I'm moving on, but I do feel like I'm progressing." He's older than me, and he wonders sometimes what to do with himself. He thinks that maybe he can help other people who have lost a spouse. I'm sure he can, but I don't think that's his primary ministry. It's guys like me he needs to encourage. Guys who can't imagine living what he's lived through and who actively avoid the thought of it. We need to prepare for grief. Last week John told me something that I can't get out of my head: "Life isn't short, it's eternal." That's perspective I need right now, so I will treat the ones God has given me to love as a gift and not as an environment. Through circumstances he would have never chosen, John has been pushed up ahead in the journey. He's seen things I need to see. He's had to go to the Prince of Peace with his tears. John's had to survive on hope. Grief has put the city of eternal peace on his map. That's what he's pointing me toward. Who can you point in that direction? When you encounter those who say, in their own way, "Who will pierce for me this deep dark cloud of grief, and light up again, as out of a clear sky, the bright ray of peace?" what will you tell them?

Peace and Depression

MY FRIEND NANCY HAS known trouble in life. It began when she and her three children were abandoned by her husband. For ten years she raised her kids on her own. Then cancer hit, with a year of major surgery and treatment to follow. As she recovered, she found herself as primary caregiver not only for her children but also for her mother through the late stages of Alzheimer's disease. Working full time was a necessity, even after her youngest son contracted debilitating Crohn's disease. When the migraines started, she wasn't surprised—they just added onto the pile of misery. Though a faithful Christian, Nancy was being driven by circumstances and exhaustion into dark and fearful valleys where panic attacks began to come with paralyzing frequency. Less than three years short of retirement she was forced to quit her job and seek hospitalization just to survive. It was there that she formally entered the world of depression.

There may be no greater peaceless void than depression. If you are reading this chapter with personal interest, you may be prone to or even engaged in the battle of depression. You don't have to have been diagnosed with depression to struggle with depressive tendencies. But please don't diagnose yourself. Don't place a label on yourself or let others do so, unless they are qualified to determine if you have a depressive disorder.* All people have sad times and depressed feelings; it is very important that you not treat

---

*If you want to learn more about depression and how you can detect it and seek help if you think you are struggling with it, go to the National Institute for Mental Health website (http://www.nimh.nih.gov/health/publications/depression/complete-index.shtml). If you are a Christian,

something that is an expression of normal life losses and disappointments as abnormal. But sadness can last longer, penetrate deeper, and close in on us in ways that begin to define who we are and how we live. That is the world of depression.

The world of depression has been described in vivid ways over the years:

> A murky vapor rises from the depths of the soul and interposes
>   itself between desire and life (André Gide, *Isabelle*);
> Rage spread thin (George Santayana);
> Lost at sea, washed between hope and despair, hailing some-
>   thing that may never come to rescue us (Julian Barnes);
> A prison where you are both the suffering prisoner and the
>   cruel jailer (Dorothy Rowe);
> The dark night of the soul (St. John of the Cross).

My friend Nancy talks about her depression as simply "this terrible dark pit."

If you have experienced depression, you are not alone. Statistics show that up to one in four people will experience some degree of diagnosable depression in their lifetime. Great leaders have not been spared depression—Abraham Lincoln and Winston Churchill changed history under its burden. Imagine the arts without the contributions of the following depression sufferers— greats for whom only one name is needed: Michelangelo, Mozart, Rachmaninoff, Dickens, Tchaikovsky, Tolstoy, Twain, Degas. Heroes of the faith have not been spared, either. Martin Luther and Charles Spurgeon and even Mother Theresa had profound and lonely battles with depression even as they gave their lives in tireless ministry.

There are some important things you need to consider about depression.

The experience of depression occurs along a spectrum. Depression isn't a "have or have not" experience. The current clinical diag-

---

please also talk about your struggle with a close trusted friend or pastor. There are spiritual dimensions to the struggle with depression that secular resources often do not consider.

nostic guidelines for depression distinguish not only types of depression, but severities as well.

The impact of depression is a whole-person experience. Deep depression not only has profound impact on a person's emotions and thinking capacity, it interacts with sleep, eating habits, and overall ability to function and focus in life.

The causes of depression are complicated and highly debated. Current research is unsettled on how depression occurs. Genetic propensities, brain chemistry, past experiences, present environment, relational deficiencies, stress levels, crisis events, physical health, and other factors are all in the mix of causal conditions. Nancy's depression seemed to develop as a number of these factors collided.

Nancy didn't wake up one morning and say, "Wow, I think I'm depressed." She didn't go for her annual checkup and get a bonus diagnosis from her doctor. In her words, she "spiraled into depression." Most people who experience profound depression describe it as something they fall into, or something that comes upon them. In *Prozac Nation*, Elizabeth Wurtzel's memoir of depression in her twenties, the author vividly describes how a person can find herself in depression:

> Slowly, over the years, the data will accumulate in your heart and mind, a computer program for total negativity will build into your system, making life feel more and more unbearable. But you won't even notice it coming on, thinking that it is somehow normal, something about getter older, about turning eight or about turning twelve or turning fifteen, and then one day you realize that your entire life is just awful, not worth living, a horror and a black blot on the white terrain of human existence. One morning you wake up afraid you are going to live.[1]

Because the cause of depression is so unclear, treatment philosophies vary. The problem with treating depression as simply a medical problem is that there is only so much medicine one can take before medicine becomes part of the problem. When Nancy was hospitalized, she was put on six antidepressants at once, which, she said, "threw my hypothyroid body into a tailspin." The problem with treating depression simply as a thinking/feeling problem is that there can be significant physical issues which contribute to the struggle—sleep disorders, chronic pain, life stresses, aloneness, debilitating illnesses, etc. Spurgeon's depression often manifested during attacks of gout. The problem with treating depression as simply spiritual is that normal spiritual activities and pursuits don't necessarily prevent it or take it away. Nancy fell into her depression even as she was doing all she knew to live as a productive Christian. As counselor Ed Welch has said, depression is a "stubborn darkness" that can afflict even the most spiritually sincere believer.

The point I'm making is that there isn't some moral line that makes depressed people a special category of sinner. Maybe the most helpful description of depression I've seen is that it is "embodied emotional suffering."[2] Depressed Christians are not "relost sinners." But depression is not a sinless suffering. Within the struggle of depression is a root struggle with sin. Ed Welch identifies the insidious drive of depression as a relentless worship of self.

> Everything turns inward in depression. A beautiful flower momentarily catches your attention, but within seconds the focus bends back into your own misery. You see loved ones who are celebrating a recent blessing, but before you can synchronize your feelings with theirs, you have doubled back to your own personal emptiness. Like a boomerang that always returns, no matter how hard you try, you can't get away from yourself.[3]

Sin is missing the mark. It is worshiping something that is not God rather than worshiping God himself. Underlying depression is a committed worship of self that nothing seems to penetrate. Nancy's self-focus tended to be a chronic comparison of herself with others, where she always came out the inferior person. In depression, one's view of oneself can become fixed and unmovable. I have seen people who can conjure no emotional response to anything in their lives suddenly flash white hot anger when they feel their internalized self-assessment is questioned. Depression will protect self against any other rival god.

For the Christian, battling depression brings with it an additional burden—the sense of being rejected by God. It goes something like this: "This faith that is supposed to transform lives has done nothing for me. God is perfect; it can't be his fault. So it must be me. I am beyond saving. Why would he even want to keep trying? I've failed God, and he's fed up with me." While we want to be careful not to read modern understandings of depression back onto biblical characters and biblical texts, this experience of spiritual desolation, which is the Christian's particular agony in depression, is woven into the poetic themes of the Old Testament. Perhaps no place do we see it more relentlessly presented than in Psalm 88:

> I am counted among those who go down to the pit;
>   I am a man who has no strength,
> like one set loose among the dead,
>   like the slain that lie in the grave,
> like those whom you remember no more,
>   for they are cut off from your hand.
> You have put me in the depths of the pit,
>   in the regions dark and deep.
> Your wrath lies heavy upon me,
>   and you overwhelm me with all your waves. Selah. (vv. 4–7)

Eighteenth-century pastor John Newton describes this spiritual despair in the depression of his niece. Elizabeth Catlett was like a daughter to him, raised by the childless Newtons since her early years. After John's wife Polly died, Elizabeth was his constant companion into old age. When she began to descend into depression, Newton was profoundly burdened. In a heart-wrenching letter to a friend, he described how Elizabeth had contracted a physical illness that, according to Newton, "had given Satan an open door to fill her imagination with horrible thoughts concerning God and his word. He persuades her that all her former religious profession was hypocrisy; that the Lord has now deserted her, cut her off, and set her up as a mark of his endless displeasure."[4] Mary's depression grew so severe that she was institutionalized in the infamous Bedlam hospital for the deranged. However, the Lord graciously intervened, and she was restored to spiritual and physical health. She eventually married and served the Lord for the remaining thirty years of her life.

With all we don't know about depression, there is one thing we do know. Where there is depression, there is no peace. But as we have seen, Jesus Christ has come to make peace and to give us peace that the world cannot know. Isn't he the one who said, "Peace I leave with you; my peace I give to you. Not as the world gives do I give to you. Let not your hearts be troubled, neither let them be afraid" (John 14:27)? How do we access this peace that will calm the troubled and fearful heart of depression? Where in the Bible can we find a path to peace?

Often people tell us that depression means we don't really understand God's love for us. But as we see from Elizabeth Catlett's sad story, God's love can just appear to be something else that has failed in our lives. It might be helpful to think about a tangible expression of God's love that can show us what it means, regardless of what we think or feel. I believe that the metaphor of God as Shepherd can be a source of comfort and vision in the darkness of depression. This is a rich and consistent description of God throughout the Scriptures; an abiding awareness of the particular care of God for the weak and wandering can be found with God our Shepherd. It has the added benefit of being a virtually obscure concept to most of us. We may know about sheep—at least the slow, dirty, and helpless part of their existence. That's something we can identify with. We can see ourselves as sheep. But we bring very few preconceived ideas into our understanding of the shepherd. We may be a little more willing to let the Bible educate us without arguing against it from negative personal experience. If we are going to find peace in depression, why not let the Shepherd lead us there? And there is no better place to learn about the Shepherd than the Twenty-third Psalm.

Even those casually acquainted with the Bible are familiar with Psalm 23. This familiarity can actually help us. We don't have to think too hard—this is not complicated theology. But it is beautiful and surprisingly deep theology, presented in a visually evocative narrative poem. The psalm is attributed to David, who grew up a shepherd. The common perception of this psalm places David pondering God on a grassy hillside overlooking his flock, which is placidly grazing in the pasture under David's watchful eye. That's probably not the setting. Most scholars believe this psalm was written under duress, possibly as David was fleeing the rebellion of his own son Absalom, a name in tragic irony meaning "my father is peace."[5] The psalm in this context is a brief scribbled journal entry of David, reminding himself that as his world is crumbling around him, there is a way out of this place he never thought he'd be. Can you identify with David in his despair? If you can, you just might find the hope he left for us in this poem. Let's walk through it slowly and thoughtfully, verse by verse.

Verse 1: The LORD *is my shepherd; I shall not want.*

Depression does very troubling things to our view of God. No matter how close we have felt to him in the past, in depression God becomes just one other thing that is against us. But from the get-go in this psalm, that perception is challenged. The God who is my Shepherd is the Lord, One "who is because he is" (see Ex. 3:14). This is the highest name God can give himself. What's more, he allows this name to be used only in connection with the promise to save. When we read "the LORD" in our Bibles, we know two things. This is the all-powerful God of the universe, and he is intensely, personally invested in my welfare. How is that expressed? He is my Shepherd. Did I choose him? No! He chose me. Sheep don't search out shepherds. Shepherds take ownership of sheep. Depression causes us to wonder if God even knows or cares who we are or what is going on in our lives. We need to confront depression and tell it, "You can darken my world and oppress my hope. But you cannot take me from the One who owns me." Jesus has said, "The good shepherd lays down his life for the sheep. . . . I am the good shepherd. I know my own and my own know me" (John 10:11–14). Who is your shepherd? Is it Jesus? That means you have been chosen by God. The price paid for you is the blood of the Good Shepherd who is now risen and reigning over all, with you particularly on his mind.

"I shall not want." That can be troubling. Depression has a tendency to supermagnify what we don't have and cloud what we do have. If you want to create a communication disconnect with people who are in depression, try reminding them of all the good things that are going on in their lives. Every possible blessing is a reminder of what is still missing, or what is about to be lost. Depression isn't a half-empty cup; it is a bone-dry canteen in the middle of the desert. A little good news will evaporate before it ever has a chance to quench thirst. But remember David's circumstances—he was a king, but he was desperately in need of help. All of his kingly resources were insufficient for his present troubles. In depression, what we depend on for our sufficiency has completely given out. Depression is a revealer of what we tend to trust in life. That's why depression so often follows loss—the loss of a loved one, the loss of a role in life, the loss of a dream. "I shall not want" is not a stand-alone statement. It points us toward how the Good Shepherd will supply our needs when all we have is need. The Shepherd is with you because he is committed to meeting the needs of the sheep. That's what he does. He wouldn't be there for any other reason.

Verse 2: He makes me lie down in green pastures.
He leads me beside still waters.

Sheep have a stubborn tendency to find a place that gives them a sense of comfort and familiarity and then simply stay there, even after the field is barren and the pool is dry. The job of the Shepherd is to move the sheep against this tendency so they don't starve; and sheep don't like to be moved. Depression has a way of reproducing this stubborn tendency in our lives. Forward movement stops. We don't like how we got here, and there's no place we can see that's any better. So we just settle in. Sleep, or at least the bed, becomes our refuge, a finite geometric space where we can cover ourselves in our misery. Or maybe it is the television, or the Internet, or just sitting in a dark place. These things can provide temporary refuge, but they don't meet our need. In fact, they entrap us if they become the center of our world. Coping with life by habitually grazing in barren fields will impoverish your soul.

To have a Shepherd means having someone who is moving us to other places, green pastures and still waters—these are images of peace. The Shepherd will never let you stay too long in your comfort zone. There is no rest there for you. The Good Shepherd has told us why he moves us along. "I came that they may have life and have it abundantly" (John 10:10). Do you trust his ability to get you to a place of peace? Trust is simply being willing to look up from false comfort to see where the Good Shepherd is leading. Ed Welch has great counsel here:

> You must do battle at this point with depression's tendencies to-
> ward passivity. Don't wait to have faith inserted into your heart.
> Seek the Lord. If there is any guarantee in scripture, it is that he
> will reveal more and more of himself to those who seek him.[6]

Verse 3: He restores my soul. He leads me in paths
of righteousness for his name's sake.

The word *soul* here is not just that "spiritual" part of us that responds to religion. Depression is a whole-person experience that requires a whole-person remedy. The idea of the soul here is a whole-person identity—who we are from the inside out. Depression has a tendency to become an identity—"I am a depressed person. I am incapable of returning to what I once was. I must

just cope with this me that I've become." But depression isn't an
identity; it is a battle of the soul. To say that the Good Shepherd
"restores my soul" means that we have a soul needing restoring,
and a means of restoration. D. Martyn Lloyd-Jones's book *Spiritual
Depression* has helped many a struggling soul over the years. Like
all books on suffering, it needs to be read with a heart prepared
to listen, because DML-J addresses not only things he thinks depressed people need to ponder, but also what they need to act on.
One of the things we need to ponder and act on is that we must
not accept things about ourselves that the Bible doesn't accept. We
must fight to align our self-view with God's view of us. Lloyd-
Jones lays it on the line: "There is nothing so uncomfortable as
clear-cut Biblical truths that demand decisions."[7] One uncomfortable truth is that the Good Shepherd doesn't negotiate the terms
of our restoration.

The Shepherd has a restoration path that he defines for us, a
path of righteousness. We walk it not because it is part of a depression treatment plan, but "for his name's sake." The beginning of
Nancy's restoration happened as she confronted the uncomfortable
truth that God was in the midst of her suffering, and he wasn't
bringing it to an end. This truth, hard as it was to deal with, actually began to produce tiny steps of faith. In all her trials, she was
actually on God's righteous path for her life.

> Throughout that year, I began to share my prayer journal entries
> that I was keeping with a friend. We both noticed that I would
> start each entry or prayer request with the words, "Lord, I am
> worried," "Lord, I am afraid." Fear and worry about the future had
> turned into anxiety, which was draining my adrenalin, depleting
> the serotonin in my body, and the final stage had turned into deep
> clinical depression. I did not fully understand what it meant to
> just sit at the feet of God and let him change my life. I did not
> fully understand until later what the Lord was doing with me as I
> was in this terrible dark pit and could not get out. I began to read
> the psalms and discovered David's frustration, fear, and sadness in
> dark places. I looked up the words "fear," "anxiety," and "worry,"

and found that it was actually a command in God's word to "do not" do those things. But "how" was the question!

The "how" for Nancy would come over time as she yielded control of her life to the leading of the Shepherd. He knows the path for us and the pace we need to follow. Friend, if you struggle with depression, you will live resistant to decisions and change. You will fight to hold on to your depression because it seems safer than anything else. But you are not depression. You are a precious soul in need of restoration. And the Great Shepherd has given his life so that you may have yours back.

> He himself bore our sins in his body on the tree, that we might die to sin and live to righteousness. By his wounds you have been healed. For you were straying like sheep, but have now returned to the Shepherd and Overseer of your souls. (1 Pet. 2:24–25)

Verse 4: Even though I walk through the valley of the shadow of death, I will fear no evil, for you are with me; your rod and your staff, they comfort me.

This verse is often used to encourage those who are facing death, or to comfort the grieving. That is a wonderful application of it. But the image is not of an endpoint, but of an environment. Commentator Timothy Laniak translates it as the valley of "deadly shadows."[8] The image of this verse is one of passing through a place known to be filled with predators and enemies. The sheep, whose only defense is a physiology that gives them heightened awareness of danger around them, are in a place they don't want to be, but can't get out of alone. They feel trapped in imminent danger. If depression is anything, it is a terribly fearful place to be. In recent years much has been made of Abraham Lincoln's lifelong battle with "melancholy" and how this might have shaped the character of the Great Emancipator. Lincoln knew the deadly shadows. He wrote in a letter:

> I am now the most miserable man living. If what I feel were equally distributed to the whole human family, there would not

be one cheerful face on the earth. Whether I shall ever be better I can not tell; I awfully forebode I shall not. To remain as I am is impossible; I must die or be better, it appears to me.[9]

Some, like Lincoln, are able to channel the deadly shadows of depression into productive activity. But even this won't lift it. For most people, it is this vague fearfulness lurking in depression that torments most. Charles Spurgeon, robust preacher of Reformed theology, castigated his depression as a "chicken-hearted melancholy."[10]

What the psalmist wants us to know is that we are never alone in the shadows. The Shepherd is right there all the time, rod and staff in hand. Much is made of the symbolism of the rod and staff. All we really need to know is this: rod and staff are experiential reminders that the shepherd is near and in control. Sheep actually feel these tools. They are guided, disciplined, freed from tight spaces, and counted as part of the flock by them. Depression attributes all experiences to either an absent God or an angry God—a God who is just as likely to run from the deadly shadows as stay in them with us. But the Good Shepherd will not leave his sheep to the shadows or what lurks in them. The rod and staff always have real purpose—to keep the sheep close, and to keep them safe. The one who wields them "shall stand and shepherd his flock in the strength of the Lord, in the majesty of the name of the Lord his God. And they shall dwell secure, for now he shall be great to the ends of the earth. And he shall be their peace" (Mic. 5:4–5).

One of the most significant ways the Shepherd makes us aware of his presence is through the faithful care of brothers and sisters in Christ. Depression tends to demand a lot from friends, and some friendships don't weather the storm well. If you struggle with depression, keep in mind that relationships are a gift, but not the answer. A faithful friend will not be a perfect friend. But they will be a friend who keeps your eyes on the Shepherd. Nancy had a faithful friend, Betsy, who called her nearly every day for a year reminding her that God would never leave her or forsake her; that he had her in the palm of his hand. The fact that Nancy would never agree with Betsy's confidence didn't stop Betsy from speaking. Eventually Nancy began to grasp what Betsy was saying. Betsy wasn't trying to convince Nancy of how much she loved her. She didn't offer herself out as Nancy's peace. What Betsy was doing and saying reminded Nancy that the rod and staff of the Shepherd were there for her good.

Verse 5: You prepare a table before me in the presence of my enemies; you anoint my head with oil; my cup overflows.

Winston Churchill described his depression as a "black dog" that harassed him unmercifully. Depression can fixate on the perceived enemies around us. The deadness of emotions, the lack of meaningful connection with others, the debilitating weariness, and the negative mental feedback loops are some of the enemies that lurk in the shadows of depression. Often enemies can't be driven off; they are with us for life. A tragic loss, a foolish choice, abuse as a child, a physical limitation, and other life tragedies shape who we are as people. David's enemies weren't going anywhere. He had them till the day he died. Some were excruciatingly painful attackers. Betrayal, regret, failure, and rejection marked his life.

But right in the middle of whatever torments us, the Shepherd sets up "a picnic" (in the words of Sinclair Ferguson)![11] This imagery of the table and the oil and the cup is typically reserved for celebration of victory. The Shepherd doesn't toss us some carrots to be eaten on the run. He puts together a banquet right in the midst of the worst enemies imaginable and then says, "Who wants to eat?" Ferguson goes on to make the point, "This is no ordinary shepherd. His ways are not our ways, his wisdom is not our wisdom."[12]

Do you have God figured out? Do you have ready objections that defeat every promise of God that you read or hear? Is depression giving the illusion that you have God pegged, that there's nothing he can do or say to change anything that matters? Prepare to be confused. The Shepherd did something very unexpected in Nancy's depression—the last thing she ever thought would happen.

In all of that darkness, God gave me a vision of how someone in my condition needed to have someone walking beside them. But I wondered how I could possibly ever do that when I could not even be strong enough in my own life. In outpatient therapy I began to notice a woman with a walker who had suffered years of depression due to many acts of abuse in her life. My heart instantly went out to her, and I felt God was saying to me, "Here she is—the woman who needs someone to stand by her." Session after session I would feel the tremendous pain in her heart but wonder how I possibly could help her. Eventually I got the courage to strike up a conversation, which led to a friendship and then the opportunity to stand with her as a mentor. During this time, my depression was lifting as well. After a year, I was able to easily go off the one medication I had taken and have never had to go back on it. I finally learned that every second of my life is under God's control even when things look so dire.

My ministry with the woman I met was truly a miracle for both of us. She began to attend church with me, and through a class we had for people exploring Christianity for the first time she grasped the truth of the gospel. Her life became full and joyful, and God had brought her to a full understanding of his love for her. Never again did she go into depression, even a few years later when she was diagnosed with advanced colon cancer. Her surgeries were unsuccessful, and she finally chose hospice to care for her in her final days. Through it all, I witnessed God's incredible peace and acceptance in her to the very end.

He had used the hardest part of my life to bring me to the most meaningful time of my life. His power would be all I would need because on my own strength or part strength, I could do nothing—but with him, all things were possible.

Friend, if that is not a table in the presence of enemies, I don't know what is.

Verse 6: Surely goodness and mercy shall follow me all the days of my life, and I shall dwell in the house of the LORD forever.

Depression says that despair is tracking me and moving in for the kill. But the psalmist is rejoicing as he moves forward. The Good Shepherd is bringing provisions of goodness and mercy to weary sheep. We don't have to go looking for it. Phillip Keller, in his classic meditation on this psalm, *A Shepherd Looks at Psalm 23*, offers an interesting view from the fields. In the world of sheep herding, a wise shepherd who leads his flocks well will actually leave a place in a better way than he found it. Keller writes:

> In a few years a flock of well managed sheep will clean up and restore a piece of ravaged land as no other creature can do. . . . In other words, goodness and mercy had followed my flocks. They left behind something worthwhile, productive, beautiful and beneficial both to themselves, others and me. Where they had walked there followed fertility and weed free land. Where they had lived there remained beauty and abundance.[13]

If you are battling depression, can you conceive of a day when you will be one whose life radiates beauty and abundance? You don't need to figure out how to get there. You have a Shepherd who knows the way. You just need to listen for his voice . . . and follow. Nancy has learned to follow.

I believe that in the "dark night of the soul," our Lord is working to make sure we know—no matter what we experience in life—that his power, love, and strength will always be with us, no matter how weak we are. And it will be used as a testimony to others who see us resting in that knowledge. The dark night of the soul becomes the dawn of peace in our lives when we allow God to be God for us.

The Good Shepherd certainly has no doubt as to where his sheep will wind up: "My sheep hear my voice, and I know them, and they follow me. I give them eternal life, and they will never perish, and no one will snatch them out of my hand (John 10:27–28)."

Nancy has peace for the future because she knows the destination. She knows she will dwell in the house of the Lord forever. She will be forever counted among the flock of God. Her confidence is not in her own strength or faithfulness; none of us can get there on that merit. We are added to the flock because of the merit of the Shepherd who chose us and lays down his life for the sheep. In your deepest despair, know that he not only owns you and is close to you, but he has been a lamb in despair as well. His despair and his travail, his dark night of the soul, was for one reason: that you might dwell in the flock of God forever. And because he has accomplished his task, all who are living in the pit of depression can look up and see that "the Lamb in the midst of the throne will be their shepherd, and he will guide them to springs of living water, and God will wipe away every tear from their eyes" (Rev. 7:17).

> Now may the God of peace who brought again from the dead our Lord Jesus, the great shepherd of the sheep, by the blood of the eternal covenant, equip you with everything good that you may do his will, working in us that which is pleasing in his sight, through Jesus Christ, to whom be glory forever and ever. Amen. (Heb. 13:20–21)

If you are reading this in the midst of despair of any kind, let me invite you to look for your Good Shepherd. He is truly near, and he is abundantly able to bring you real peace.

Peace and Conflict

IN THIS STUDY ON peace we've covered how the shalom of God that was meant for us was lost and then restored through the life and work of the Prince of Peace. We've seen how this peace is meant to function for us in some common and deep struggles with life in a fallen world. Now we are going to take a final turn and begin to see how shalom is meant to affect our relationships with others. This chapter will focus on how we deal with situations where peace is broken by conflict. In the next chapter we'll see how we can promote the peace of God among our brothers and sisters in the church. And finally we'll look at what it means for God's people of peace to take that peace into a world in serious trouble.

Conflict Is in the Air

It was our fifteenth anniversary. My wife and I had farmed out the kids in several directions, packed our bags, made the mad dash to the airport, and were now sitting at the gate catching our breath. We would soon board a flight west, to begin an adventure at a Rocky Mountain resort we'd been dreaming of and carefully planning for months. On the way to the gate I'd noticed a Cinnabon stand in the terminal. Once we were settled, my thoughts went back to that stand and the sublime and addictive treats that entice sugar addicts like me. I couldn't resist: "Honey, I'm going to get a Cinnabon, do you want one?" "No," Jill replied. "I'm not hungry." I was back shortly with my Cinnafix in its nice little Styrofoam cocoon. It's important to note that serious Cinnabon eaters always eat from the outside in—toward the "heart" of the bun, where the intense goodness is most highly concentrated.

As we sat there waiting for our plane, I was having one of those "this is how it should be" moments—excitedly talking about the upcoming adventure with my beautiful bride and enjoying one of my favorite treats. As we chatted, I began to notice that my beautiful bride had begun encroaching on God's good gift to me, poaching bits of my Cinnabon with her fingers. Why be annoyed, I thought—even though she already turned down one for herself. She is my wife, and this is our anniversary, and everything I have is hers. What are a couple of bites off my treat? I got up to check the flight status, and when I returned, I discovered that she had eaten the very heart out of my precious Cinnabon! I couldn't believe it. How totally selfish and uncaring of my needs! After trying to deal with my hurt quietly, I came to the conclusion that, if our trip was going to be meaningful for our marriage, I needed to be honest. I needed to tell her how much her selfishness had wounded me. So I did. Her response shocked me. She didn't see anything wrong with what she had done!

Everything she said after that—saying she was sorry, offering to buy me another one—seemed patronizing. She completely missed the point of her offense. She needed to see how she had wounded me with her uncaring ways, which were made all the more egregious by the fact that we were celebrating our anniversary. So I shared that truth with her as well. She then had the audacity to take offense at my assessment of the situation. She actually got angry with me! For an entire three-hour flight to Denver, we tried every conflict resolution scheme we knew— broad moralizing, bringing up past failures and weaknesses, stating and restating our opinions, the silent treatment—nothing we put into play worked. The only thing we could agree on was that our anniversary was getting off to a lousy start. Conflict had rudely disrupted the way things ought to be.

Just to put you at ease, we were able to get past that conflict, and we had a wonderful anniversary with no further turmoil that we can remember. But I tell the story because it highlights something important about the peace-disrupting experience of conflict. Conflict occurs and, sadly, endures because we are willing to settle for less than peace in our relationships. When conflict threatens, we may want to win, we may want to have our feelings acknowledged, we may want to establish blame, we may want to fix a perceived problem, we may want to pretend like nothing is wrong. But anything less than the goal of peace will not produce peace. Things will not be the way they are supposed to be.

You might be thinking, "If the best you've got is a Cinnabon spat, then you have no idea what conflict is really like." Friend, let me assure you, we've had worse conflicts in our marriage, and I've been in worse outside it. As a counselor, I have also seen conflict in its ugliest forms. I've seen people who are willing to destroy everything valuable in life just to get their way. What we need to see is not how bad conflict can get; we need to see that in every conflict there is an absurd commitment to things that destroy peace. Only by identifying and addressing these antipeace commitments with gospel remedies can we resolve conflicts and restore shalom in our relationships. We're going to take a look in this chapter at a wonderful passage of Scripture that can help us set the goal of peace in every conflict and employ the means that the Prince of Peace has given us to reach that goal.

Let the Peace of Christ Rule

The apostle Paul wrote a letter to the church in Colossae—a church he probably had never met. It is a letter of encouragement and practical instruction, much like his more expansive letter to the Ephesians. But one distinct issue he addresses with great concern is the presence of false preachers and a false, hyperspiritual teaching in the church—problems that are producing considerable controversy and conflict among the people. The letter begins with an expression of great confidence in the power of the gospel among them (Col. 1:6) and a heartfelt pastoral prayer for them in light of that power

(1:9–14). Paul then goes after the false teaching. He draws their gaze upward to the majesty and transcendence of Christ himself, and how the transcendent Christ has reconciled them to God, not through imparting mysterious knowledge, but by shedding his own blood. "For in him all the fullness of God was pleased to dwell, and through him to reconcile to himself all things, whether on earth or in heaven, making peace by the blood of his cross" (Col. 1:19–20).

Paul contends against the false teaching by calling the Colossians to trust nothing but the gospel, live out nothing but the gospel, and reject anything that is not in keeping with the gospel. It is the gospel, and only the gospel, which is able to keep them secure (Col. 2:6–15), united (2:16–19), and holy (2:20–23). Having addressed the presenting problem in the church, he then turns in chapter 3 to instruction on how gospel community should be lived out even in the midst of controversy and conflict. While peace *per se* is not the main point of this text, we'll see how God's shalom is woven implicitly and explicitly throughout Paul's words. Let's take this passage and break it down with application to the conflicts in our lives.

3:1–4: Shalom Is Our Highest Aspiration

> If then you have been raised with Christ, seek the things that are above, where Christ is, seated at the right hand of God. Set your minds on things that are above, not on things that are on earth. For you have died, and your life is hidden with Christ in God. When Christ who is your life appears, then you also will appear with him in glory.

Paul begins by taking us back to his great christological declaration in 1:15–23: "If you have been . . ." The resounding answer is, "Yes, we have!" How? As we see above, we have been reconciled to God through the cross; we are alienated people who have been made holy and blameless before God (1:21–22). To be raised with Christ, to be hidden with Christ in God, is shalom. Paul appeals to us that we settle for nothing less than all we can have in the shalom of Christ Jesus.

3:5–11: How Shalom Unravels into Conflict

Put to death therefore what is earthly in you: sexual immorality, impurity, passion, evil desire, and covetousness, which is idolatry. On account of these the wrath of God is coming. In these you too once walked, when you were living in them. But now you must put them all away: anger, wrath, malice, slander, and obscene talk from your mouth. Do not lie to one another, seeing that you have put off the old self with its practices and have put on the new self, which is being renewed in knowledge after the image of its creator. Here there is not Greek and Jew, circumcised and uncircumcised, barbarian, Scythian, slave, free; but Christ is all, and in all.

Shalom unravels when we exalt our cravings (Col. 3:5–7). Unfortunately, our natural tendency is to settle for far less than shalom in Christ. Seeking and setting our minds on things above doesn't come naturally. In fact, what comes naturally is seeking and setting our minds on anything else than what is above. In his familiar terminology, Paul draws a hard line—we are called to put to death (the term is very strong in the Greek) what is earthly, as opposed to what is raised with Christ (3:1). He offers five particular human tendencies as expressions of "earthiness"—*sexual immorality, impurity, passion, evil desire,* and *covetousness* (3:5). What is significant about these examples is not what they are individually, but what they are collectively. These are all desire/want-driven motivations that are deeply embedded in our hearts. We may hide them well from others, but they root within us nonetheless. We know they are sinful because they invite the wrath of God (3:6). What you have here is Paul's psychological model; the shalom in our lives is not broken by our circumstances, by the actions of others toward us, by genetic propensity, or by unmet needs. Shalom is broken by our desires in full-hearted pursuit of things that cannot satisfy our true needs. That's what *idolatry* means in verse 5.

The apostle James affirms Paul's diagnostic.

What causes quarrels and what causes fights among you? Is it not this, that your passions are at war within you? You desire and do not have, so you murder. You covet and cannot obtain, so you fight and quarrel. You do not have, because you do not ask. You ask and do not receive, because you ask wrongly, to spend it on your passions. You adulterous people! Do you not know that friendship with the world is enmity with God? Therefore whoever wishes to be a friend of the world makes himself an enemy of God. (James 4:1–4)

There's that word *enmity* again—remember chapter 2? Where cravings rule, enmity abounds. When our hearts pursue the earthly/worldly, we turn away from the shalom God intends and open a new rebellion against God and his ways. The first step in addressing conflict is to look at the source of it—the cravings of our own hearts. Counselor and author David Powlison describes what God does to kill off the false idols in our hearts so that we may seek the things above, where Christ is.

> The deepest longings of the human heart can and must be changed as we are remade into all that God designed us to be. Our deviant longings are illegitimate masters. Even where the object of desire is a good thing, the status of the desire usurps God. Our cravings should be recognized in order that we may more richly know God as the Savior, Lover, and Converter of the human soul. God would have us long for Him more than we long for His gifts. To make us truly human, God must change what we want; we must learn to want the things Jesus wanted.[1]

In my conflict with Jill, identifying the cravings below the conflict wasn't easy. I was blind to my own cravings for respect and physical gratification (a dangerous combination in a man), even as I thought I saw hers with laser clarity. But somewhere over the Midwest the Spirit graciously began to bring awareness of my idolatry—not clarity, but a glimmer that the source of the conflict just might be me. Without the Spirit, I would have never seen it any other way. When I began to turn away from what I wanted, I started to see what God might want for me.

Shalom unravels when we exert our demands (Col. 3:8–9). If our sinful cravings are truly the problem, it would seem that the simple answer would be just to keep them to ourselves. Paul anticipates that strategy and informs us that cravings inevitably express themselves in outward actions—words and deeds that incite conflict. If you wanted to start an all-conflict team, you couldn't find better players than the roster Paul drafts: anger (think looking for a fight), wrath (hair-trigger temper), malice (obsessing over wrongs done to you), slander (no limits on what you say or who you'll say it to), obscene talk (verbal attacks) and, that crowd favorite, lying (seeing yourself entirely as a victim). I'm confident that thoughout the three hours of our transcontinental Cinnabon conflict, I put all of these players in the game. When I think that I acted like such an enemy to my wife on our anniversary over such a little thing, I still cringe. But I'm not surprised. I had a point to make, a battle to win. When cravings are allowed free range in our lives, we will act on them. And when we do, we will have conflict.

The good news is that we don't *have* to act out our cravings toward others. We have "put on the new self, which is being renewed in knowledge after the image of its creator" (3:10). Contrary to most conflict resolution strategies we hear about, which seek to simply repattern or rechannel desires into more constructive behaviors, we have the grace and peace of God in our hearts working against our fleshly cravings. Angry people can choose by God's grace not to act in anger. When we are tempted to nurse grudges or shoot off a sarcastic text, there is an activity of God at work changing us. As we put to death worldly cravings and seek and set our minds on things above, our lives will increasingly promote peace and quench conflict.

Shalom unravels when we erect relational walls (Col. 3:11). As we saw in chapter 3, reconciliation with God through the atonement of Christ has produced a new people—a people whose unity in Christ is greater than any division or diversity of race, ethnicity, or social standing. That unity had happened to the Colossians, but it was being undermined by the division arising out of the false gospel they were hearing. Old prejudices were coming back into play; folks seemed to be taking sides. In times of conflict we can find comfort in identifying with those who seem most like us. When business is tough, employees side with each other against management (and vice versa). When the team hits a losing streak, you start to hear murmurs about "those guys" over on the other side of the locker room. When marriages are in conflict, extended families tend to schism along blood relations. Sadly, churches and denominations often fall into this tendency (we'll address this in the next chapter). Conflict becomes "me against you" or "us against them." The casualties of conflict are felt in every level of society. Listen to this frank assessment of conflict from the work of the Arbinger Institute, a secular international conflict resolution organization:

> Look around. Home and workplace casualties are everywhere. Bitterness, envy, indifference, resentment—these are hallmarks of the hot and cold wars that fester in the hearts of family members, neighbors, colleagues, and former friends the world over. If we can't find the way to peace in these relationships, what hope do we have for finding it between nations at war?[2]

Paul's words are a plea to reject the fleshly divisions that undermine the unity of God's people. Notice that in Paul's descriptions of various factions, everyone has some group that conveniently can be the bad guy for their problems. Jews have their Greeks, Greeks have their barbarians (and the barbarians even have their Scythians—really barbaric barbarians!). If you put three people in a room and let them loose in their cravings, eventually you will have two in cahoots against one. You may be able to achieve a truce, but there will be no peace. It is in the nature of the sinful world to divide. But in Christ there is unity and shalom. Only in Christ is there "all in all."

3:12–14: Preserving Shalom in the Threat of Conflict

Paul now provides a prevention plan against conflict among God's people:

> Put on then, as God's chosen ones, holy and beloved, compassionate hearts, kindness, humility, meekness, and patience, bearing

with one another and, if one has a complaint against another, forgiving each other; as the Lord has forgiven you, so you also must forgive. And above all these put on love, which binds everything together in perfect harmony.

Put on the grace that suppresses conflict (Col. 3:12). Firefighters will tell you that no two fires are alike. The materials that combust in the fire, the ignition material, the environmental conditions, surrounding areas that can be affected, and the collateral damage potential are all factors that must be considered in fighting a fire. Over the years a number of different fire suppression materials and techniques have been developed to fight fires according to their unique characteristics. The common goal of all suppression systems is to extinguish a fire where it occurs and, where possible, prevent a fire from igniting or reigniting.

There is a fire-like quality to human conflict. Conflict can erupt suddenly and do tremendous harm before it is extinguished. Proverbs 26:21 says, "As charcoal to hot embers and wood to fire, so is a quarrelsome man for kindling strife." Even after it's over, the damage of conflict can remain in relationships. As with fires, the best approach to dealing with conflict is prevention, or as one fire company has said it, "Learn not to burn." In contrast to the lists of sinful "fire starters" that Paul has told the Colossians to get rid of, he now offers a list of "fire suppressers." When these are present in our lives, it will be very difficult for conflict to erupt in our relationships.

Compassion is the disposition of a heart toward mercy. Mercy causes us to look for some way to extend grace to a person who might do something that could tempt us into conflict.

Kindness is a fruit of the Spirit that will not respond to evil with evil, but will look to do good in whatever situation we encounter.

Humility is a profound awareness of our own weakness and unworthiness before God that makes it difficult for us to exert our demands or personal sense of "rightness" on others.

Meekness is a gentleness that is careful in all circumstances to not affect others in a negative way, or tempt them in their weaknesses.

Patience is the capacity to absorb the wrongs of others against us without retaliation.

I think if even one of these virtues had been functioning in me as I was eating my Cinnabon, Jill and I would have never spent our flight in a stupid argument. What all of these conflict suppression virtues have in common is that they are expressions of the character of God that we are called to display. They are available to us as gifts of grace. As God's "holy and chosen ones" we have the call and the means to reflect what he is to others. That will suppress conflict and promote peace.

Sadly, however, on this side of heaven we will struggle to put to death the things that incite conflict and fail to walk in the grace to suppress conflict. Like Jill and me in our low moments at high altitude, you will find yourself in conflict looking for a way out. For times when we do find ourselves in conflict, Paul now offers us two gospel-empowered conflict resolution strategies that can restore peace to relationships.

Bear with one another (3:13a). The threat of conflict presses an immediate question upon us: How do I respond to what feels like an offense against me? I faced that question when I discovered the missing middle of my Cinnabon. Jill faced it a few minutes later when my "honesty" came to her in the form of accusation. At this moment, everything in us naturally wants to either fight or flee. Either one classifies as conflict. But Paul offers a third option. We can bear with someone. We can absorb others' actions or words or attitudes against us and not respond in kind. This isn't the same as allowing someone to walk all over us or setting "boundaries" so that someone's behaviors don't affect us. Bearing with one another is an application of the mercy of God that we have received. (Read and reflect on Psalm 103 if you need a fresh awareness of God's mercy for the undeserving.) The fact that Paul says bear with "*one another*" should help us. For all the bearing we do with others' offenses, we can be confident that someone is actively bearing with us. Bearing with one another can have a powerful effect on what happens in relationships. Had either Jill our I chosen this path, our next few hours would have looked profoundly different. Bearing with others is often the wise approach to difficult situations. Proverbs 19:11 says, "Good sense makes one slow to anger, and it is his glory to overlook an offense." Think of conflicts you've had recently. How many of them could have been averted had you simply chosen to bear with the other person—chosen not to say that last comment, not to make that face, asked a question rather than made a statement, or asked to pray rather than offer a piece of your mind?

It isn't always possible to overlook offenses. How do we know when to overlook and when to address an offense? Pastor Alfred Poirier employs a two-day test:

> If I find myself frequently reflecting on my brother's or sister's sin for more than two days, if it is there when I rise and when I go to sleep, if I think about it when I'm showering and when I'm driving, and if I'm reticent to greet this fellow believer at church, then I cannot overlook the offense. I must address the matter with the person.[3]

In his book *The Peacemaker*, Ken Sande offers some important counsel on when we shouldn't overlook an offense but rather go to the other person. We shouldn't simply overlook an a offense

> when it is dishonoring to God;
> when it is damaging to our relationship with that person;
> when it is hurting others;
> when it is hurting the offender.[4]

Note that the choice of whether we bear with or address offenses is not a toss-up decision. The choice of bearing with the offenses of others is determined by what best promotes God-pleasing peace.

Forgive one another (Col. 3:13b). There is simply no greater asset to peace in a world of relational sin than forgiveness. Yet it is one of the most misunderstood aspects of the Christian life. When I meet with people in conflict and we get to the point where they want to resolve the conflict, I'll ask them to confess and forgive one another. Almost every time this is what I hear:

"I'm sorry that what I did upset you."
"That's ok. Don't worry about it."
"Thanks."

Now there are far worse things that could be said, but as a counselor I can't let that pass for forgiveness. Forgiveness is holy—it is the privilege and call of people whose sins have been paid for by Christ. Alfred Poirier is right to say, "Forgiveness is a divine gift and work. It is part and parcel of the Messiah's restoration of the cosmos."[5] To reduce it to simply apologizing or "getting on the other side" of a conflict is to do nothing short of reducing the gospel to an appeasement strategy. If you have sinned against someone, you need forgiveness—from God and them. If someone has sinned against you, forgiveness isn't an option; Paul says the forgiven must forgive. Forgiveness is the intentional covering of one person's offense by the offended party. It is the complete and permanent release of a debt owed, or a sin committed. The goal of forgiveness is reconciliation, the restoration of full and unhindered peace in relationship. The cost of forgiveness is that the one sinned against is willing to bear some effect of the offense to let the offender go free. That is hard and often painful work. But there is no better way to live out the gospel than to give and receive forgiveness. Here are some gospel affirmations to stir your faith toward forgiveness.

- In the gospel I have been reconciled to God and live as a minister of reconciliation to others (2 Cor. 5:18–19). Therefore I can approach all my conflicts looking for God's reconciliation purposes for me in them.
- In the gospel I have forsaken my own righteousness for the righteousness of Christ. Therefore I can see disagreement or

even the sins of others against me as opportunities to die to myself and glorify God.

- In the gospel I find my identity in my union with Christ. Therefore I am able to please God no matter what another person does to me. In conflict the actions of another person never need to define me or determine how I act.
- In the gospel I have been forgiven of the guilt for my sin. I can confess sins I commit knowing that God will forgive me of them. Since God forgives me of my sin, I can confess it to others with honesty, clarity, and conviction.
- In the gospel I see that forgiveness comes with a price heavily paid by the one extending it. Therefore in conflict I will never trivialize the asking of forgiveness, and will never offer forgiveness without the intent of fully releasing the person I am forgiving from the debt he or she owes to me.
- In the gospel I know that God is at work in my circumstances by his Spirit to make me more like Christ. Therefore I can view conflicts as opportunities to grow through adversity, not unpleasant interruptions in my way of life.
- In the gospel I have been called to a life of faith, hope, and love (1 Cor. 13:13). Therefore I can view conflict resolution as an opportunity to walk out the life of a peacemaker who sows peace to raise a harvest of righteousness (James 3:18).

I once heard Christian philosopher Cornelius Plantinga ruminating on forgiveness at a conference. His thoughts, as best as I could capture them, vividly express the heart of forgiveness.

Forgiveness is a journey with a definitive start, not a closure experience. To forgive, we will have to do some dying. We will have to pray our anger into the heart of God. Forgiveness is about setting certain memories out of our reach. Instead, we deliberately bring to mind that which will soften our hearts toward the other. We will focus on the value of lasting relationship. Forgiveness is a form of grace that flourishes for all parties. Forgiveness does not mean setting the clock back on the relationship (as if nothing happened). It is a turn away from destruction to a new future.[6]

In God's kindness and through Jill's patience, I was able to gradually see the foolishness of my response to her that precipitated our conflict in flight. With that sweet conviction I was able to humble myself and acknowledge my own selfishness, judgment, contentiousness, and anger in how I related to her throughout the experience. Jill was happy to thoughtfully forgive me and release me from the burden to try to undo all I had done. As we taxied toward the gate in Denver, reconciliation was taking place and we really did turn away from destruction to a new future. We've had to walk through this confession/forgiveness drama many times in our marriage—exchanging parts depending on whose sinful cravings are most engaged—but God has never failed to meet us with redemptive grace and reconciling peace.

Doing confession and forgiveness is never easy. I have found that there are four really hard things I need to say—somehow, some way—if I am going to do my part in resolving conflict. These are never things I feel like saying, but grace seems to always bring them uncomfortably to mind. The next time you find yourself in a conflict, see if you can bring these things to mind—and then find a way to usher them out of your mouth.

"I was wrong."

"Do you see anything else that I might not be seeing?"

"How did this affect you?"

"Will you please forgive me?"

And if you are on the receiving end of these kinds of statements, you have the opportunity to extend generous forgiveness.

If we are going to embark on the journey of forgiveness, whether that journey begins with confession of our sin against another or receiving confession from another (and over time we'll have to do both), there are some things we need to prepare for prior to conflict. We need to commit to eliminating any other options for dealing with conflict that don't involve at some point the personal and verbal confession of sin and the personal and verbal granting of forgiveness. We need to commit to dying to personal vindication. Someone else admitting wrong does not prove that we are right. Only God is absolutely right; only he is holy. Vindication of me can never be bundled with forgiveness of you. And we need to prepare everyday for future opportunities to forgive. Trust me, if you wait until you hear someone's confession to gather the motivation to forgive them, you will never hear a confession that motivates you to forgive. No one will ever adequately confess away the pain of a sin against you. We prepare to forgive others in the future by dwelling on how we've been forgiven in the past, in short, by pondering regularly, if not daily, the gospel of peace.

What ultimately preserves shalom in conflict is love (Col. 3:14). The power to put to death sinful cravings that drive conflict is love. The power to resist sinful actions and words that ignite conflict is love. The power to break down walls of separation is love. The power to bear with and overlook the sins of others against us is love. The power to wait however long it takes for your offenses to be addressed by the person who offended you without judging them is love. And most assuredly, the power to walk out forgiveness when we have sinned or been sinned against is love. Love, whether extended in forbearance or forgiveness, covers a multitude—a numberless crowd—of sins (1 Pet. 4:8). Love is the crowning grace, the grace of graces, that will keep relationships clothed in peace.

Peace That Passes Conflict

> And let the peace of Christ rule in your hearts, to which indeed you were called in one body. And be thankful. Let the word of Christ dwell in you richly, teaching and admonishing one another in all wisdom, singing psalms and hymns and spiritual songs, with thankfulness in your hearts to God. And whatever you do, in word or deed, do everything in the name of the Lord Jesus, giving thanks to God the Father through him. (Col. 3:15–17)

It is easy to read Paul's closing words in this passage as wishful thinking. Sure, Paul, I'd love to let peace rule, and walk around all day singing praise songs, always doing everything in God-pleasing ways. Isn't that what heaven is for? But right now things are messy. My relational world is full of strife and problems. Life is complicated.

Yes it is, and that's exactly why Paul wrote this letter. He's a realist. He knows that peace doesn't just happen. We have to work on it daily. So he says, let the peace of Christ rule. Shalom isn't a goal, it is literally a "governor" that is meant to guide our decisions and actions in relationships along the road that love sets out for us. Among all the other things that would rule our relational world, we empower peace to its ruling status by allowing the word of Christ—the gospel—to dwell in us richly. The deeper the gospel penetrates our hearts, the more the Peace of Christ will govern our actions. What will result is a relational world where disagreement happens but it is handled with wisdom rather than conflict. The sweet aroma of thanksgiving and praise will permeate our times together. It is not insignificant that the Prince of Peace called his people to be reconciled from conflict before they come together in worship (Matt. 5:23–24). He is determined that all relational experiences—be it congregational worship, personal friendship, or family dynamic—be governed by peace and overflowing with thanksgiving. Conflict will occur, but shalom is meant to be the norm—a norm that can be returned to again and again through love. In this way, whatever we do, "in word or deed," can be done "in the name of the Lord Jesus, giving thanks to God the Father through him" (Col. 3:17).

For God's people in a world of strife, that's the way things ought to be.

9

Peace and God's People

I LOVE GOING TO Apple Church. It's such a peaceful place. My Apple Church is in one of the largest malls on the East Coast. To get there is a pilgrimage—fighting traffic, the exhausting search for a distant parking space, the long mind-numbing trek past all manner of kiosk barkers and storefronts enticing you off the narrow way. But finally arriving at Apple Church is worth the travail. Entering through a wide, square archway, you are enveloped in the quiet sanctuary that is Apple Church. No loud music, only the hushed sounds of fellow Appleites also seeking tranquility from the harsh world outside. Everything is a pristine, holy white. It is somehow not sterile, but comforting. For white is the festal color of Apple. As you move through the sanctuary, you become aware of the deep worship around you. Small clusters of fellow pilgrims pay rapturous homage to iCons in small chantry areas throughout the cathedral. An iMac chapel here, an iPad chapel there—the faithful reverently speak to one another in iPsalms, iHymns, and iSpiritual songs. There are no PC pagans here; we are all iWorshipers. Though we all have different conversion stories, a deep unspoken unity exists among the fellowship.

At the far end of the sanctuary is the Great Altar, behind which are the Apple Priests, each busy with his or her own sacerdotal duty. Yet they are graciously attentive to the needs of the flock. You approach the altar with a certain trepidation because you know that the moment you open your mouth, the secrets of your computing soul will be known to all. Whether you are there for counsel on the deeper mysteries of Apple or confession of a computing sin, or whether you desire healing for your Mac, you must prepare yourself for the liturgy of the priests. If you do well, you may understand a third of what is said, so far higher is their knowledge than yours. But these words are computing life, offered freely to the faithful, and you drink them in with a glad heart. At the end of your audience, you genuflect, give thanks, and turn to leave. But you don't want to go back into the world of the mall, because there is comfort in this place. This is your congregation; they welcome you because you share the most important thing—Apple. Here at Apple Church we are equal, even if our iPhone isn't the latest version available. Because you are Mac and that means you belong. There is always peace at Apple Church.

Keeping Peace with the People of God

Wouldn't it be nice if our local church experiences were like Apple Church? A place of peace and order where we could escape the chaos of the world and just worship God with our loving brothers and sisters. Isn't that what the church is supposed to be?

Unfortunately, we know all too well that the church is not always a haven of peace. No one joins a church looking for conflict. But it doesn't take long before we experience some type of conflict. It might be a disagreement over worship practice, Sunday school curricula, a change in leadership, a new direction in outreach, a family squabble that goes public, or how the church handles its budget. There is truly no limit to what church people can argue over. Conflict happens in churches because churches are congregations of sinners—redeemed, yes, but not fully sanctified. We're still working this love and holiness thing out in practice. Conflict happens because we care about the church and what it stands for, sometimes enough to fight about it. When things that are important to us seem to be under attack, it is a natural response to want to defend them. Conflict also happens because the church has an enemy, and one of his best weapons is division (Eph. 4:26–27). And conflict happens simply because mistakes and misunderstandings happen. People do well-intentioned things that don't work out, or they say ill-considered things that are taken the wrong way, tempting us to divide over perceived offenses.

Unfortunately, when peace is broken by conflict in the church, things can get ugly quickly. We don't tend to do conflict resolution any better than we do conflict avoidance. Conflict in the church leads to factions, church splits, denominational division, power plays, no-confidence votes, lost trust, bitter feelings, and broken relationships. Sadly, it also leads to a degrading of the church's witness in the culture. All too often what people know most about a church are its conflicts. There's an oft-told joke about a guy who has been discovered on a deserted island, where he has built three huts. One is his home and one is his church. When asked about the third hut, he replies, "That's the church I used to go to." The humor in this story is sadly in its familiarity. Where conflict erupts in a church, of any size, there will be no shalom.

One might reasonably think to look to the New Testament church and its example to find out how to keep peace in the church. But we really won't find the peaceful church model we're looking for there. Nearly every letter included in the New Testament addresses in some way active conflict in the church. Some of the problems might seem familiar to you. Division over doctrine? Check out Colossians, 1 and 2 Timothy, 2 Peter, 1 and 2 John, and Jude. Denominational problems? See 2 Corinthians. Legalism and license controversy? Galatians is all about it. Arguments among leaders? That's Philippians. Controversial behavior among the saints is addressed in 1 and 2 Thessalonians and Ephesians. Of course, the mother of all conflict letters is 1 Corinthians, where Paul has to address all of the following problems: disagreements over preaching style, disputes over leadership, immoral behavior, Christians suing each other, marriage and divorce controversy, worldliness debates, financial management, evangelism strategies, gender roles, liturgy, spiritual gifts, and eschatology.

But these problems with conflict don't disqualify the New Testament writers from addressing conflict. In fact, it was God's sovereign intent to use the problems of the early church to provide his church throughout the ages with inspired wisdom for promoting and maintaining the peace of Christ in his church. A powerfully succinct expression of that wisdom is found in the third chapter of the letter of James.

Wisdom and Peace

The author of this letter is James, the half brother of Jesus and the first acknowledged leader in the inaugural church in Jerusalem. In reading through the book of Acts, it is clear that James had to work through a number of potential conflicts and disturbances in the early Christian community. Most significantly, it fell to James to navigate the church through what is probably the greatest controversy the church has ever known. Did Jesus come just to the Jews or to the whole world (see Acts 10–15)? All of church history flows out of how this controversy was ultimately resolved. The letter of James was most likely written to predominantly Jewish churches which sprang up as the first generation of believers was dispersed out of Jerusalem by persecution. It is a letter that addresses how Christians should walk in faith when faced with trials from without (persecution) and within (factions and dissensions). At the very center of the letter, James summarizes his vision for the believing community: "And a harvest of righteousness is sown in peace by those who make peace" (James 3:18). The question we want to consider is, in the church, where conflict is common, how do we make peace? Here's what James has to say:

> Who is wise and understanding among you? By his good conduct let him show his works in the meekness of wisdom. But if you have bitter jealousy and selfish ambition in your hearts, do not boast and be false to the truth. This is not the wisdom that comes down from above, but is earthly, unspiritual, demonic. For where jealousy and selfish ambition exist, there will be disorder and every vile practice. But the wisdom from above is first pure, then peaceable, gentle, open to reason, full of mercy and good fruits,

impartial and sincere. And a harvest of righteousness is sown in peace by those who make peace. (James 3:13–18)

We are going to look a little closer to James's instruction here and then make some practical application for how this can play out in our church involvement.

Wisdom from Below Undermines Peace (James 3:13–16)

The context for James's words above is an extensive warning on the complexities and perplexities of speech in relationships (3:1–12). Beginning in verse 13, he drills down to the core of the issue, which is wisdom. James's use of *wisdom* is drenched in proverbial overtones; wisdom is a practical outflow of our worship. Whatever we fear (worship) will determine how we live. Theologian Graham Goldsworthy sums up Christian wisdom this way: "Wisdom is a theology of the redeemed man living in the world under God's rule."[1]

The necessity of the wisdom James is making an appeal for stands in contrast to the alternative—what he calls *earthly, unspiritual, demonic* wisdom. Wherever it comes from, earthly wisdom is not good stuff. The characteristics of this wisdom are a true threat to the relational world of God's people. "Bitter jealousy and selfish ambition" are a tag team of sinful motivations that produce what one commentator describes as a "spirit of harsh, abrasive self-concern" that easily gives "rise to inability to tolerate and get on with others."[2] You'd like to hope that this kind of toxic blend could be contained, but it never can. As another commentator notes, what results from this earthly wisdom, in James's view, is that a "party spirit forms a group which emotionally or physically withdraws from the rest of the church."[3] The inevitable result is "disorder and every vile practice" in the church (3:16). The word translated "disorder" here is the same word Paul uses to address the contentious Corinthians: "For God is not a God of confusion [disorder] but of peace" (1 Cor. 14:33). In other words, there is a way for people to act in the church, a way that seems very natural and reasonable to them, that in fact is the opposite of what God wants. It opposes his purpose in the church and destroys the shalom that should characterize his reconciled people.

Wisdom from Above Promotes Peace (James 3:17–18)

Having presented a very unappealing way of doing church, James then offers God's way—the "wisdom from above." James unfolds this wisdom in a list of virtues that, while not taken from the lists that Paul offers, clearly maps onto the same terrain as the "fruit of the Spirit" (Gal. 5:22–23) and virtue lists other apostles present. When we encounter this wisdom list, we need to try to put ourselves into the mindset of proverbial wisdom. In other words, rather than seeing each of these virtues as a stand-alone goal that we can check off when we reach it, we need to see them as characteristic of someone who is motivated by wisdom from God. If our greatest concern is the honor of God (which is nearly always the declared goal of any person in church conflict) then our words, actions, and choices will look like what James describes: "first pure, then peaceable, gentle, open to reason, full of mercy and good fruits, impartial and sincere."

Let me do some straight talking here. Maybe you've been involved in a conflict in the church. Maybe it was something personal; maybe you or a family member were treated in a way you felt was un-Christian. Perhaps you've felt judged by others, or that somehow the church wasn't there for you in the way you needed it. It could be that you've been involved in a controversy over a doctrine or practice in the church, something you believe is very important to the church and its mission. Or maybe you're a leader who is on the outs with another leader. In whatever conflict you've been in, here is the question you can't avoid: How have your words, actions, and decisions lined up with wisdom from above? James doesn't give a middle way here. And he doesn't start by validating your perspective about others. He goes for the heart—your heart. Either we walk in earthly wisdom (with its inevitable destruction) or wisdom from above. Let's not demean the peace of the church by justifying what we do as "standing on principle" or "obeying your conscience." Everybody who is involved in a church split or divisive controversy thinks they are standing on principle or upholding conscience. Interestingly, the more divided we get, the more confident we tend to be that we are righteous in what we're doing. James is not naive—that's why he puts "pure" at the head of the list. All the other aspects are the way "first of all pure" will be lived out. Only God is the definer of pure. Before we decide that a certain action or comment is *necessary*, we must ask, is it *pure*?

The beauty of this list is that it doesn't hinge on who is right and who is wrong. If you are right in a dispute (in some objective way), you can walk out your rightness in wisdom from above. If you believe you are unfairly accused of something, you can properly respond with wisdom from above without having to simply "give in for the sake of peace." If you feel you've exhausted all remedies on your end to peacefully resolve a situation, you can make appropriate decisions that will provide for future opportunities for reconciliation without burning relational bridges. Not all disagreements are bad. Doctrinal clarity and mission focus are often worked out through disagreement. That's the story of church history. Sometimes in the mystery of God's providence he will advance his kingdom agenda through separations (we see that in the parting of Paul and Barnabas into separate missions after years of productive partnership [Acts 15:35–41]). And, of course there is the all encompassing promise that "for those who love God all things work together for good, for those who are called according to his purpose" (Rom. 8:28). These words should take on special meaning when we find ourselves disheartened by conflict with our brothers and sisters in the church.

I recently observed a demonstration of peaceful disagreement play out on the Web. A spoken-word artist posted a video of himself speaking one of his poems on the Internet. The video went viral, generating hits in the millions in a few short days. It contrasted worshiping Jesus against religion and apparently struck a chord with a lot of people who loved the "not religion" sentiments that were expressed. A well-known Christian leader blogged about the content of the poem, offering a thoughtful critique. He raised the question of whether the antireligion parts weren't a straw man that were more divisive than helpful. The Internet public, as it is wont to do, quickly divided in two camps, supporting either the artist or the blogger. What's remarkable is that in the midst of this sudden whirlwind of controversy, the blogger and the poet were engaging in humble gracious dialogue, seeking to understand one another and commend one another wherever possible. It was a testimony of how two men demonstrated, in a very public forum, the wisdom that comes from above.

However, all too often we throw the shalom of God under the bus of our own worldly agendas for the church, and then justify our means to get what we believe are God's ends. James will have none of it. "A harvest of righteousness is sown in peace by those who make peace" (3:18). Here is the point I believe James is making: There is no "right outcome" of any problem in the church that can justify the destruction of the shalom that has been bought so dearly by the blood of Christ. Whatever side we are on in a disagreement or problem, we had better be about the work of peace if we hope to end up on the side of God. This can be extraordinarily difficult in the passions of church life, but there is no greater work we can do. We simply must make it our supreme goal in every situation. Do you want things to be right in the church? Be a peacemaker.

For the rest of the chapter, I'd like to work this peacemaking wisdom down to the street life of our local churches. In every church there is one constituency with two interrelated parts. Every church is a people and its leaders. To draw from biblical Greek, an *ecclesia* and an *episcopos*. How these two entities work together make up the mission and ministry of the church. So let's look at an application of peacemaking for each entity—the people of the church and its leaders.

Peacemaking among the People—
Eliminate Gossip and Slander

To me, the single most destructive force in the church is the tongue. I have seen churches go through massive changes and problems and emerge on the other side strong and faithful because there was a maturity in the congregation regarding how people talked about problems. I've also seen churches torn apart over the smallest and most picayune disagreement or problem because people chose to employ their tongues in gossip and slander. As we've already observed, James comes after the tongue with gusto. In its destructive power, "the tongue is a fire, a world of unrighteousness . . . set on fire by hell" (3:6). James isn't an opponent of free speech. He's hammering an essential theme of wisdom that is woven throughout the book of Proverbs. Consider this vivid advice:

> Whoever meddles in a quarrel not his own
>   is like one who takes a passing dog by the ears.
> Like a madman who throws firebrands, arrows, and death
> is the man who deceives his neighbor
>   and says, "I am only joking!"
> For lack of wood the fire goes out,
>   and where there is no whisperer, quarreling ceases.
> As charcoal to hot embers and wood to fire,
>   so is a quarrelsome man for kindling strife.
> The words of a whisperer are like delicious morsels;
>   they go down into the inner parts of the body.
> Like the glaze covering an earthen vessel
>   are fervent lips with an evil heart.
> Whoever hates disguises himself with his lips
>   and harbors deceit in his heart;
> when he speaks graciously, believe him not,
>   for there are seven abominations in his heart;
> though his hatred be covered with deception,
>   his wickedness will be exposed in the assembly.
> Whoever digs a pit will fall into it,
>   and a stone will come back on him who starts it rolling.
> A lying tongue hates its victims,
>   and a flattering mouth works ruin. (Prov. 26:17–28)

James isn't alone among the apostles in his concern for the effect of the tongue in the peace of the church. Paul addresses the issue in several churches (2 Cor. 12:20; Eph. 4:31; 1 Tim. 5:11–13), and Peter makes this heartfelt appeal for protecting and pursuing peace through guarding the tongue: "For 'whoever desires to love life and see good days, let him keep his tongue from evil and his lips from speaking deceit; let him turn away from evil and do good; let him seek peace and pursue it'" (1 Pet. 3:10–11).

There is no greater concern regarding the tongue than the issue of gossip and slander. They are often found together (Ps. 15:1–3; Prov. 20:19; Rom. 1:29–30) and are related sins against shalom. The root idea behind gossip is that of "whispering," saying things (about people) that the people you are talking to don't really have a right or need to know. The motivation to gossip is almost always to share unflattering things about someone else. As Bertrand Russell said, "No one gossips about other people's secret virtues."[4] Slander is usually understood as speech against another person with the intent of degrading them to others. It is probably best not to sharply distinguish the two, because where one is, the other is also likely in operation. Gossip and slander wage war on the very things that build peace in the church. Rather than tether us together, they divide us. Rather than build up, they tear down. Rather than testify, they defile. Where gossip and slander exist in the church, there will always be disorder and every evil practice. Here are some very important things to grasp if we are going to guard the peace of the church in the face of gossip and slander.

We can't plead innocence over our gossip and slander because we didn't mean to do any harm. Have you ever sat around talking about life in the church, telling stories with good friends about experiences, and found yourself getting a good laugh about a friend who just happened not to be there? Did you ever find yourself in a situation where everyone was talking about problems in the church and this or that leader who is the problem behind the problem? If you've had these kinds of experiences, you have most likely sinned in gossip and slander. Whether one has a premeditated *intent* to spread gossip or to slander someone is not the only issue; sometimes it's not even the primary issue with these sins. What constitutes gossip and slander is its *effect* on others or in the church. If we speak or participate with others in a way that creates negative impressions or distrust in the church, we are gossiping and slandering. Ignorance or "I didn't mean to" is never a free pass.

We can't plead innocence over our gossip and slander because we spoke in factually correct ways. Often the most damaging gossip and slander is based, at least in part, in truth. In a society driven by information and dissemination, this is increasingly becoming a problem for the church. We think we have a right to know whatever information we feel we need to know, and anything other than complete disclosure and availability of information is tantamount to spin control, if not outright deceit. People or websites that leak or publish information that can damage the reputations of others (regardless of facts) from the lofty perch of "truth" are in fact gossips and slanderers with no valid biblical defense for their actions. There is no inherent need to know or report things that are not our direct concern, and where we believe we have a direct concern, passages like James 3:17 must guide and govern how we give and receive information.

We can't plead innocence over our gossip and slander because we have a right to voice our opinion. This is another emerging challenge within the church as we engage a world of instant communication. The postmodern mindset and the Internet have unleashed a self-expression explosion unparalleled in history. Everyone who has an opinion about something (and who doesn't have opinions?) now assumes an unfettered right to share it—a cardinal virtue is postmodern culture. Communication technology and portals (blogs, e-mail, instant messaging, texting, and posted video are the prevailing means as I write this) hype up this value to compulsive dimensions. Whatever I have going on inside me—in my brain, in my guts—needs to be expressed RIGHT NOW. No more caution over knee-jerk responses and unformed evaluations. And what I have needs to go somewhere "out there." No more private journals where I work out my struggles in reflective quiet. The great generic world of Digital You needs to know in an unfiltered way what Digital Me is feeling in real time. This is a wildly combustible combination that never promotes peace. There is no cultural limit on what we say, who we can reach, or our right to say it. But there is a God who hears every word, reads every post, and receives every tweet, and he evaluates it according to his standard of purity. The Lord can work in our hearts to help us deal with ungodly thoughts toward others, but once they are expressed, we own the sin of them—to him and to whoever is affected by them in the world around us.

We can't plead innocence over our gossip and slander because we didn't pass on gossip that we've heard. Gossip and slander are communal sins. There must be a giver and a receiver. Passively receiving gossip and slander from someone is participating in it. Often what undermines the peace in a church is not the few who gossip and slander, but the many who receive and tolerate it. I am not recommending that we squelch open dialogue in the church, but there is a biblical call to guard the church against division and the people who stir it up (Titus 3:10). Here is a truly practical way to do peacemaking in the church. If someone comes to you with gossip or slander, love for them and for the person(s) they are talking about should include gentle, merciful, and sincere admonition to turn from it and seek to undo any damage the gossip may have caused. This is sowing in peace that will raise a harvest of righteousness.

Note that in each admonition above, I talk about "our" gossip and slander. I have experienced the sting of gossip and slander against me, but sadly I have also been part of the gossip and slander train myself. When I've realized I have gossiped or slandered, I've tried to own the wrong, but I haven't been able to undo the effect.

As people in the congregation, let's commit to walking out wisdom from above in our speech. Let's value *purity* by committing to speak in ways that honor God above all things. Let's be *peaceable* by looking for ways to heal division when we see it. Let's practice *gentleness* by being considerate of what's best for the person we're talking to. We can be *open to reason* by looking for the value in the perspectives of others, even if we disagree with them. Our words can be *full of mercy and good fruits* when they are motivated by compassion and the desire to be a blessing whenever we open our mouths. A great way to be *impartial* is to resist taking sides in a conflict wherever possible. And we can be *sincere* by working in all relationships and disagreements to preserve trust and good will among our brothers and sisters.

It was said of Winston Churchill that he "mobilized the English language and sent it into battle."[5] Do you see your words that way? In your home, with your friends, in your fellowship group? When your words go into battle, what side are they on? Are they on the side of division and strife and discord? Or are they on the side of peace? No matter what is going on in your church, there is no situation that requires us to just say what we feel or think. And there is no situation that cannot be handled best by wisdom from above.

Peacemaking for the Leaders—
Handling Departures in Peace

I believe one of the best and most neglected ways pastors and church leaders can practice peacemaking is when someone decides to leave the church. It's inevitable that church leaders will, at some point, engage with someone who has been a faithful member of the church but then struggles with the church and considers leaving. Sometimes these members have been our long-time friends and fellow laborers. No matter what the reason for their decision, considering leaving a church can be a very difficult issue. People build their lives into good churches; their time and money and gifts and families become interwoven into the fabric of the church we lead. When they feel the need to leave, it is likely to be an agonizing experience for them. Usually the thought of leaving isn't sudden; it has grown over time based on various experiences that may be unrelated to each other. A relational loss here, a change in church direction there, a ministry vision not fulfilled, misunderstanding with a pastor, a new church starting in the area, etc. These are just a few of the issues that can coalesce in the decision to leave a church.

No matter what the reason, people who leave their churches can experience unexpected and dramatic changes in their lives. Long-standing friendships will change, maybe even end, if for no other reason than it's hard to keep relationships going when you're not building a life together. Kids ask why, and parents don't have easy answers. Well-meaning people who hear that others are thinking of leaving feel that to leave is a loyalty breech and take it personally. Others who may be nursing grudges of their own with the church seek them out and press their own issues into the mix. The "leave or stay" dilemma is a trial that can vex the souls of godly people. They sit down with us leaders, and it all spills out. And we are caught off guard, unprepared for the intensity test. Their rationale seems flawed and their attitude seems wrong, and we are at the heart of all their problems. So we try to reason, and that sounds defensive. We try to help them with their souls, and that sounds like we're turning the tables. Or we try to offer them a clear way out, and that feels like rejection.

Sadly, dear folks sometimes leave their churches with a bad taste in their mouths. They are all alone, vulnerable to other struggling people, vulnerable to the crazy commune of the Internet, vulnerable to spiritual drift. They may become what they didn't want to be—spiritually indifferent at best, but often struggling with bitterness as well. And as time goes by, they don't know how they got where they are. It just all went wrong. And two years, or five years, or fifteen years of their Christian experience goes into an "I don't know what that was all about" file.

Pastor, what is it like to leave your church? What can we do to be peacemakers when people leave? Here are some principles I've tried to apply over the years.

We can encourage people to love Christ's church, not just our church. In our new-members class, one of the things we stress over and over again is a desire to help people learn how to find and participate in a gospel-preaching church, whether we become that church for them or not. We can humbly acknowledge that we are not the ultimate expression of doing church. That's hard because we are doing the best we can to make our church all it can be. I try to keep a ready and up-to-date list of our church weaknesses in my mind. I want to be able to agree with people who perceive legitimate weaknesses. Do you know what people might find difficult about your church? If we are fluent in our weaknesses, we'll be less likely to react to people when they point them out.

When members do come with the declared intention of leaving, we can try to follow a meaningful pastoral path. Here are some things I try to do. Make sure the first thing they hear is our profound appreciation for them coming and talking to us. Don't treat the interaction as an opportunity to persuade them to stay. And don't formalize it as an "exit interview." Make a sincere effort to listen and hear, not in a "let me get this straight" way, but in a way that will allow them to honestly say, "I think you are hearing and trying to understand where I'm coming from." Clearly and warmly express that if they leave, they will be deeply and personally missed—by the leaders and by the rest of the church body. Make an appeal for a dialogue because of the importance of the decision *for them*—a dialogue that wouldn't simply be about whether they stay in the church but about how we can learn and grow no matter what they decide.

If they decide to leave, make sure they know that you are committed to do everything you can to help them find a new church home. Even if someone leaves, I try to schedule follow-up calls or meetings to find out how the process is going. I've had more than one family settle back with us when they looked around and realized that our church (with its acknowledged flaws) was as good as they might find elsewhere. Make a commitment to lead the way in appreciation, affection, and trust in God for them so that no one in the church will question that they are valued brothers and sisters whether they stay as members or not. Keep a door open for care until they settle somewhere—stressing that if trials come when they are between churches, you are there for them. Make an intentional follow-up of prayer and friendship that allows them to continue to talk about their concerns even if they are not under your care. Some of my most valued advisors are folks who were with us but now have an "outsider" perspective.

Clearly there is a limit to what we can do to work through departures—some folks' struggles can make it very difficult to walk together or part amicably. But we're talking about peacemaking that seeks the fruit of righteousness. Let's approach our departing brothers and sisters in the spirit that the apostle Paul commends: "Finally, brothers, rejoice. Aim for restoration, comfort one another, agree with one another, live in peace; and the God of love and peace will be with you" (2 Cor. 13:11).

The Call for Churches of Shalom

Theologian J. Gresham Machen was no stranger to controversy and division, having been at the center of the orthodoxy and modernism debates of the turn of the twentieth century. He even lost his ordination in the Presbyterian denomination over his stand for essential Reformed doctrine. Machen was a fierce opponent of any idea or movement that would undermine the gospel and a faithful friend to all who sought to preserve it. Like many great reformers in church history, Machen's was not a placid personality—he was a fighter for truth to his final breath. But in many ways the purpose of his fight was for peace in the church. In a time when the dominant trend in major churches and denominations was to accommodate the prevailing ideas of the day, Machen and his friends desperately tried to preserve a church where the true peace of God could be found and promoted in the lives of its people. At the end of his book *Christianity and Liberalism*, Machen offers a plea for the church that James and the other apostles and God's people throughout the ages can amen:

Is there no place of refreshing where a man can prepare for the battle of life? Is there no place where two or three can gather in Jesus' name, to forget for the moment all those things that divide nation from nation and race from race, to forget the puzzling problems of industrial strife and to unite in overflowing gratitude at the foot of the Cross? If there be such a place, then that is the house of God and the gate of heaven. And from under the threshold of that house will go forth a river that will revive the weary world.[6]

Let us now look to that river in our final chapter and how peace is meant to flow through us to the culture in which we live.

Peace and My World

Peace on Earth?

Angels are a big part of my childhood Christmas memories. I remember them everywhere around the house—on the tree, on the walls, and on practically every flat surface not otherwise occupied. A cherubic infestation of the holiday season. The angels around my house were always holding something. Usually it was a harp, or a star, but in every grouping there was one assigned the job of holding the scroll with the words "Peace on Earth." As a little kid I had no idea why they would choose that slogan and not something like "Obey Your Mom." Which is how seven-year-olds tend to get "peace on earth."

As I got older, I realized that the cute little seraphim were holding up a Bible verse, or at least a part of one. In Luke's account of the birth of Christ, he makes much of the declaration of the angels: "And suddenly there was with the angel a multitude of the heavenly host praising God and saying, 'Glory to God in the highest, and on earth peace among those with whom he is pleased!'" (Luke 2:13–14).

However, I really didn't know what "peace on earth" meant. Church taught me that God had something to do with it. But growing up in the late 1960s, I became aware there wasn't a whole lot of peace in my world—the Vietnam War, civil rights strife, and campus protests, not to mention considerable sibling infighting on the home front. Maybe God needed to fire the angels and go direct to market. By my early college years, I had abandoned anything resembling belief in God. To me, at that time, God was the problem, not the answer. Hearing "Glory to God in the highest and peace on earth" was ironic at best. To me, as long as there were people wanting to bring glory to God, there could never be peace on earth. Then Jesus got me. The problem was, he got a sinner, and a self-righteous one at that. For the first time I noticed that what the angels declare in Luke is "Glory to God in the highest, and on earth peace among *those with whom he is pleased!*" And I thought to myself, yeah, that's right! People like me who please God should have peace. People who don't please God don't deserve peace. For the first time I was reading the whole verse. But I still didn't get it.

Peace on earth is a confusing thing.

We've covered a lot of territory in this book. We've pondered the universal desire for peace—harmony, order, fullness—and why we wind up with strife, chaos, and emptiness instead. We've discovered the glorious remedy for our peace problem in the reconciliation between us and God that was accomplished in the life, death, and resurrection of Jesus Christ. By looking at several real-life challenges, we've seen how we can fight for the peace of God in our personal experience, in our relationships, and in our churches. But there is a world out there to which God promised peace. And it can be very difficult to see the payoff of that promise. The purpose of this final chapter is to discover how you and I, as reconciled people of God, are meant to be part of God's delivery of peace into a world in desperate need of it.

To do this we're going to have to work in an arena where there is much controversy. How does one who has received the peace of God bring it to others and model it in a world alienated from God? More simply put, how do Christians influence their world for the sake of peace? To address this we need to turn our attention from angelic declarations at Christmas to frightened disciples at Easter.

The Peace Commission

> On the evening of that day, the first day of the week, the doors being locked where the disciples were for fear of the Jews, Jesus

came and stood among them and said to them, "Peace be with you." When he had said this, he showed them his hands and his side. Then the disciples were glad when they saw the Lord. Jesus said to them again, "Peace be with you. As the Father has sent me, even so I am sending you." And when he had said this, he breathed on them and said to them, "Receive the Holy Spirit. If you forgive the sins of any, they are forgiven them; if you withhold forgiveness from any, it is withheld." (John 20:19–23)

Commentators often refer to this passage as the great commission according to John. It is filled with a wonderful tension and drama we need to ponder. It is Easter night 1.0. A little over forty-eight hours before this, the disciples had seen their Rabbi brutally crucified as a revolutionary enemy of both the state and their religion. They are a bewildered bunch, unable to comprehend the rapid and violent succession of events over the past few days. Certainly the most disorienting event of all is that Jesus is no longer in the tomb where he was laid. That much they know for sure. There is an incredible report that Mary has actually seen Jesus—alive! Is this a vision, or the ecstatic delusions of a woman overcome with grief (John 20:11–18)? John gives a clue to the mental state of these people in a telling detail: they were huddled in a locked room "for fear of the Jews." If the authorities could kill the one who calmed the seas and raised the dead, what might they plan to do with his impotent followers?

Then total shock. Jesus himself is standing among them! How he got in, no one knows. But he is here, and he speaks! "Peace be with you." A common greeting, like he's just dropping by to say hello. But these words are now filled with new meaning. The last words he spoke to them all, words of comfort in the quiet before his arrest, come flooding back to mind: "Behold, the hour is coming, indeed it has come, when you will be scattered, each to his own home, and will leave me alone. . . . I have said these things to you, that in me you may have peace. In the world you will have tribulation. But take heart; I have overcome the world" (John 16:32–33).

With that he holds out his hands and shows them his side, irrefutable proof that he has truly overcome the world. The fight for peace with God has been won by the Prince of Peace! As commentator Bruce Milne accurately states, this blessing of peace

> represented the first truly authentic bestowal of shalom in the history of the world! Precisely because he has brought the kingdom of God into realization by his death and rising, now and only now is shalom a realizable blessing. Thus his "Shalom!" on Easter evening is the complement of his "It is finished!" on the cross, for the peace of reconciliation and life from God is now imparted.[1]

Before they have a chance to take this in, Jesus repeats the blessing, "Peace be with you." But this time there is a command attached: "As the Father has sent me, even so I am sending you." And there is another action; he breathes on them. This signifies the promise of the Holy Spirit to empower their going, confirming his promises in the upper room and the garden (John 14:15–26; 16:7–14). Then there is a declaration: "If you forgive the sins of any, they are forgiven them; if you withhold forgiveness from any, it is withheld." This is a commission of power and of authority. It is time to leave the locked room and go into the world—a world of tribulation and enmity with God—and declare the message of God's blood-bought shalom to all who will hear.

This is where you and I enter the story John is telling. When those disciples unlocked that door and left that room, the world began to change. Ordinary people, sinners in fact, began to be reconciled to God. And they became part of the great plan of God to bring the message of peace with God to other lost enemies of God. We are two millennia into the process, and there is much left to be done. But it is a foregone conclusion that this message of reconciliation will accomplish its mission, because the Prince of Peace has overcome the world.

We're going to spend the rest of this chapter talking about how God intends to use reconciled enemies like us to extend shalom in this world. We will explore a plan that is broader than what we usually think of as the mission of the church, though that is crucial to the plan. The biblical concept of peace, while centered on the proclamation of the gospel, is broader than that, covering the entire experience of human culture. To finish what we started in this book, I want to offer the following Peace Plan as a way to think through our involvement in the full range of God's shalom activity in the world he has made and into which we are sent. The Peace Plan has three dimensions: a lasting mandate, an invasive mission, and a transformative ministry.

The Global Peace Plan

A Lasting Mandate

The Global Peace Plan begins with a lasting mandate. The lasting mandate unfolds from the beginning of Genesis as man and woman, made in the image of God, are given subordinate dominion over God's creation and called to populate the earth (Gen. 1:26–27). They are placed in the garden with the command to "work it and keep it" (Gen. 2:15), and Adam is to name all the animals who populate it (2:19). In other words, the shalom of the garden included man's active participation in filling, cultivating, managing, and expanding it. Theologians see this as more than simply agrarian toil; it is the birth of culture. The garden was created to be developed in such a way that the glory of God would be displayed through his precious image bearers. Human beings were to extend the shalom of God by the contribution of their ingenuity, creativity, and effort, working with the natural world God had provided for them. From the expression of these God-given abilities was to come a world of art and science, building and shaping, words and ideas, achievement and advance—all to the glory of the Creator. This is commonly called the *cultural mandate*. It was meant to bring us immense satisfaction and to bring God great joy. With the loss of shalom in Genesis 3, the purpose for culture making is lost, or, more accurately, twisted. The culture making of man follows the bent of his heart, becoming idolatrous, oppressive, and exploitative.

But God didn't throw up his hands. Throughout the unfolding story of the Old Testament—God's counterinsurgency of shalom—we see the merciful heart of God toward the misery of man. It is this heart of mercy that has preserved the world from what could happen if man were left entirely to his own sinful motivations. As bad as things are, they are not nearly as bad as they could and should be. We call this *common grace*—God's restraining care that retains the essential dignity of what he originally created. Though man's culture building has been in opposition to shalom, there has been remarkable beauty and goodness and insight displayed over the centuries and throughout the world. Arts have flourished, good deeds have been done, civilization has advanced in astounding ways. Nevertheless, corruption taints everything in some way, and many things in profound ways. The natural world, meant to be an environment of sustenance and beauty, is abused and polluted with abandon. There is constant violence and poverty, racial hatred and human exploitation. Sin abounds and all manner of evil, cruelty, and corruption play out among supposedly civilized peoples. Things are not what they are supposed to be, and God sees it all.

Common grace, however, is not beaten down. God's mercy and kindness know no bounds (Psalm 117). Furthermore, we see, woven into God's plan of shalom, a call for his people to be a blessing in the world. They are to act and create in ways that promote shalom in the culture around them. They are to stand on the side of his justice and faithfulness for the good of the larger humanity. Space doesn't allow an expansive survey of this thread of cultural concern through the Bible, but you can trace it in the full array of Old Testament declarations.

IN THE LAW

For the LORD your God is God of gods and Lord of lords, the great, the mighty, and the awesome God, who is not partial and takes no bribe. He executes justice for the fatherless and the widow, and loves the sojourner, giving him food and clothing. Love the sojourner, therefore, for you were sojourners in the land of Egypt. (Deut. 10:17–19; see also Lev. 19:9–18)

IN THE WISDOM

> By the blessing of the upright a city is exalted,
>> but by the mouth of the wicked it is overthrown. (Prov. 11:11;
>> see also Psalm 146; Prov. 14:31)

IN THE PROPHETS

> He has told you, O man, what is good;
>> and what does the LORD require of you
> but to do justice, and to love kindness,
>> and to walk humbly with your God? (Mic. 6:8; see also
>> Isaiah 58; Amos 5)

What becomes remarkable to see as we move into the New Testament period is this: The fulfillment of God's Shalom Plan in Jesus does not create a people who retreat from the problems of the world around them. In the parable of the Good Samaritan (Luke 10:25–37), Jesus makes it abundantly clear what truly religious people will do when faced with the effects of sin in the world around them. Jesus had no problem crossing social and ethnic lines for the sake of his kingdom. His own ministry was so replete with care and healing for the oppressed and sick and disenfranchised it seemed at times to onlookers to obscure the call to faith and repentance that his good deeds were pointing to—a misunderstanding that happens even to this day. He intentionally passed on his concern for justice and mercy to his disciples (Matt. 25:31–46—the "least of these" parable), and they seemed to get it. Note Paul's comments in Galatians 6:10: "So then, as we have opportunity, let us do good to everyone, and especially to those who are of the household of faith." The writer of Hebrews simply says, "Strive for peace with everyone" (Heb. 12:14).

Timothy Keller captures the essence of this biblical call to do good to everyone:

> Doing justice includes not only the righting of wrongs, but generosity and social concern, especially toward the poor and vulnerable. This kind of life reflects the character of God. It consists of a broad range of activities, from simple fair and honest dealings

with people in daily life, to regular, radically generous giving of your time and resources, to activism that seeks to end particular forms of injustice, violence and oppression.[2]

It is this activity that is in view in Jesus's summary call in the Beatitudes, "Blessed are the peacemakers, for they shall be called sons of God" (Matt. 5:9). This is not a job description that Christians are supposed to fulfill. Shalom-making in this world in all its forms is an overflow of a life transformed by the reconciling power of the gospel. Christians should do shalom as a way of life wherever they are because it is essential to who they are. I was talking to my friend and fellow pastor Ian McConnell about this, and he said something that captures the authentic Christian encounter with injustice, oppression, and moral wrong: "It's like hearing fingers scrape on the blackboard of our soul. We just want to do something to stop it."

Shalom-making, therefore, is a lasting mandate for God's people in this world that has never been rescinded. We love to do good and bring peace. There are a host of ways we may carry out this mandate; we can do many things that preserve and promote the dignity of human beings as created in the image of God and that care for the world he has created. At times, individual Christians will need to step forward to speak and act for justice when the civil rights of others, even those we may disagree with, are clearly being violated. As a Christian community we must at times vigorously register our conscience against wrongs in our culture, as when, for example, Christians march for life and the rights of the unborn. One thing we may not do is ignore or withdraw from our culture. As long as we live in this world, we will have a part to play in its preservation and good—a part given to us by God.

Let's get a bit practical. What good are you in the world? How big is your footprint for shalom beyond the confines of your faith community? As I write this, there is a wonderful trend among churches to want to freshly engage the world in its concerns and work with its institutions for the betterment of communities and cities. I know musicians and artists who are engaging audiences and peers outside traditional Christian contexts with a view to being a meaningful part of the cultural dialogue. I see the same kinds of creative engagement in the worlds of business and politics and science, where Christians are refusing to fall into stereotypical religious roles in favor of building bridges for the sake of common good. These are not easy inroads to build, and they come with temptations and possibilities for dangerous compromise. But in a culture where to be "Christian" is synonymous with being irrelevant and sanctimonious, we must not fear new thinking and edgy ideas. Things like reformations and great awakenings and evangelical revivals tend to start outside the box of conventional religious norms and forms.

An Invasive Mission

Not to contradict what I just said, but the lasting mandate isn't our entire concern, or even our chief concern. We can't let cultural impact become our mission. Historically speaking, nothing has marginalized the effect of Christians more swiftly or completely than allowing ourselves to be identified as promoters of humanitarianism and moral virtue. There is a point where new becomes wrong, and edgy falls off the table of true. Our impact is meant to be much more significant than even representing the mercy and justice of God. The nail holes and pierced side of Christ are not proof that he is willing to die for peace; they are peace themselves! The best any human being can do in common grace is promote beauty or pacify suffering and injustice in his little part of the world this side of eternity. Jesus Christ has come bringing an eternal government of peace for all who will receive him as Prince of Peace. As much as we must care about and act sincerely and diligently to arrest the wrongs of society, that is a job which doesn't require someone to be a God-redeemed shalom-maker to do. Christ has come and brought God's reconciliation, a peace initiative that is cosmic in scope. God's people are called to *proclaim* peace from God, not just reflect it. "How beautiful upon the mountains are the feet of him who brings good news, who publishes peace, who brings good news of happiness, who publishes salvation, who says to Zion, 'Your God reigns'" (Isa. 52:7).

We walk in this world promoting peace, but we are sent into this world for the sake of the gospel of peace. The apostle Paul offers us a tremendous vision of this "invasive mission of peace":

> All this is from God, who through Christ reconciled us to himself and gave us the ministry of reconciliation; that is, in Christ God was reconciling the world to himself, not counting their trespasses against them, and entrusting to us the message of reconciliation. Therefore, we are ambassadors for Christ, God making his appeal through us. (2 Cor. 5:18–20)

There is considerable scholarly debate about whether Paul here is speaking of all Christians or specifically of his apostolic ministry in Corinth.[3] But the imagery here of being an "ambassador of reconciliation" maps onto the same worldview that sent disciples from the upper room out into the world with the good news of salvation. Those who have been reconciled carry the message of reconciliation to others. We may do good in our world, but what is most significant about us is not our good deeds. It is the Prince of Peace we know and proclaim.

I'm calling this an invasive mission because it is not what the world expects or, frankly, wants. The world loves Christians who do good deeds; it persecutes Christians who proclaim good news. Jesus gives an idea of what happens when "the way things ought to be" confronts "the way things just are."

> Do not think that I have come to bring peace to the earth. I have not come to bring peace, but a sword. For I have come to set a man against his father, and a daughter against her mother, and a daughter-in-law against her mother-in-law. And a person's enemies will be those of his own household. Whoever loves father or mother more than me is not worthy of me, and whoever loves son or daughter more than me is not worthy of me. And whoever does not take his cross and follow me is not worthy of me.

Whoever finds his life will lose it, and whoever loses his life for
my sake will find it. (Matt. 10:34–39)

While the proclamation of the good news will not make us
popular, it is nevertheless the only good news for all of humanity.
The doing of justice and good in the world flows from the heart
of a sinner reconciled by grace to God. The preaching of the gospel offers that transformative reconciliation to others. The neglect
of one will distort the other. The faithful exercise of the lasting
mandate will provide opportunities for the invasive mission and
its message. The faithful carrying out of the invasive mission will
ensure that temporal improvement isn't achieved at the expense
of eternal peace. How does the gospel mission become invasive?
The invasive mission carries forward through personal witness and
community proclamation.

Personal Witness. The mission expressed in personal witness
requires us to engage in the fallen world, not separate from it.
Christians should be among non-Christians in a way that builds
relationships and creates true mutual understanding and appreciation. Why would someone want to hear from us if they felt we
disdained everything that mattered to them? We need to invite
ourselves into the culture of those who are alienated from God.
We won't be invited on our own merit. But we must be careful to
go as ambassadors—people sent representing someone else. We
need to be conversant there—not necessarily fluent. We need to
be educated there, but not enculturated. We need to cultivate influence there because we have a message that needs to be clearly
shared and demonstrated. We engage in acts of mercy and service
and build relationships looking for opportunities to witness for
Christ. This is personal evangelism, getting close enough to people
to meaningfully share the gospel with them. We're not talking
about evangelistic strategy; this is evangelistic love. Kevin DeYoung
and Greg Gilbert spell this out:

> If we are Christians whose love and compassion is aroused not
> just by physical and emotional needs, but also by spiritual needs,

then sharing the gospel will always be in the forefronts of our minds. We will naturally and readily move toward it as we are loving other people.[4]

Are you in the world positioned to witness for Christ? As a pastor I spend so much of my time relating to Christians, I have to create time to be among non-Christians. I need to work hard to get to know people on their turf in their terms. One of my goals is to find everyone I meet interesting. I want to know their stories, their thinking on things, how they process life. I want to be affected by what's important to them so that our conversation about the gospel, which is the most important thing about me, is just that—a conversation. Is there anyone you would find it difficult to talk to? A liberal? A right winger? Somebody with a GLBT T-shirt? Somebody with golf pants? Somebody with different skin color? Who is that person who, just by being who they are, you'd have no interest in getting to know? What do you need to do to overcome that obstacle? What are love and peace calling you to do?

Community Proclamation. Individuals alone cannot embody the full expression of the gospel mission. Jesus didn't set up the Great Commission that way. Because shalom is a community reality, people who receive the message must be added to the community of peace—the local church. The church represents the mission of peace in the world. It is the place where those who embrace the good news of peace find a home. Furthermore, the church is the training center and the mission base for the gospel. In our church, our evangelistic "strategy" is resolutely centered around life in the church. We encourage people to do "initiative evangelism" (just creating conversation with strangers) because God can bless it, but mostly because it gets thoroughly entrenched church people out in situations where they can see God work through them in spite of their fears. But what we really love is when Christians get to know unbelievers in their community and then, as an expression of genuine relationship, invite them into the experience of the church community—their "family of faith." As pastors we try to make our church world as accessible as possible—church is a very strange place for most people in the culture these days. By accessible I don't mean hiding hard truth; I mean putting it right out there in front of folks. We've found that people don't visit churches for palatable principles for life. They have hard questions about God and want somebody to take them seriously. That's what our churches should be: places where hard questions are welcomed and clear biblical answers are provided with humility and kindness. We can't save anyone—that's God's job. What we can do is give straight truth in gracious ways, and seek to live it out before others as they struggle to come to terms with it.

My friend Daphne can tell you about finding a home in the community of peace. A few years ago she lost her only son in a drive-by shooting—on Easter Sunday. Months of life-swallowing grief and bitterness followed. She found herself one weekend at an event at our church, hearing things about God's love and forgiveness that infuriated her. But she liked music and there was a free CD available, so she took it. It was a CD of worship songs. Though she didn't really understand the words, the music gave her a sense of peace, so she played it constantly. She started to come to church just to listen to the music. People who had no idea of her pain reached out to her week after week, and she started to feel more comfortable. Somehow the message of the gospel worked its way into her soul. She tells her story:

> Then, one day, while I was listening to the CD and crying over my son, the words of a song hit me. God's love for me was so great that he gave up his only Son. I would not have given up my son for a second, but God gave his Son for me. I asked, "God, how could you give your only Son?" and I repented of my sins and accepted Jesus's forgiveness. I felt God's love and began to realize what everyone had been talking about. I realized that Jesus had drawn me to himself by putting these people in my path to help me and comfort me—strangers, people who had nothing to gain from me.

You won't find a more grateful person than Daphne. She will always grieve the loss of her son, but she has peace, and she knows she is home.

This is why I love church planting. Church planting puts new expressions of the peace community of Christ into areas where they haven't been, or where the ones which were there have lost their effectiveness. Church planting imports witnesses and throws them into neighborhoods and businesses and sports leagues and community activities where they directly engage individuals at war with God. The mission of peace gets plopped down in the most unexpected places through church planting. It is hard work, and there are costs to the enterprise. But in my mind there is no more effective expression of the invasive mission of peace than the planting of churches.

A Transforming Ministry

Cultural commentator Andy Crouch has some great advice for anyone who wants to impact the world for God:

> If our excitement about changing the world leads us into the grand illusion that we stand somehow outside the world, knowing what's best for it, tools and goodwill and gusto at the ready, we have not yet come to terms with the reality that the world has changed us far more than we will ever change it. Beware of world changers—they have not yet learned the true meaning of sin.[5]

Friends, we will never be able to create a mission strategy that will transform the world. Our efforts to alleviate suffering and promote justice will hit monumental walls of legal regulation, entrenched opposition, and corrupt institutions. And Jesus has already told us we will be persecuted for preaching the gospel. We will get compassion fatigue and ministry burnout. We need to be sobered by the true depravity of sin. Humanity has chosen to reject peace from God and has no intention of going back. It is the sober reality of just what obstacles those who promote the cause of shalom inevitably face that will move us away from self-dependent zeal to God-dependent prayer.

Why pray? It is God's will as revealed in his Word. Prayer is the indispensible imperative for the transforming ministry of peace in the world. In prayer we have access to the power and heart of God for the good of the world. It is a power that cannot be thwarted by the strife, chaos, and emptiness of the world. As individuals and churches, when we can do nothing else, we can pray. In fact, before we do anything, we should pray. Do you want to see God glorified and the kingdom of peace extended? Pray, "Father, hallowed be your name. Your kingdom come" (Luke 11:2). Do you want to see the mission of peace embraced by more and more of God's people? "Pray earnestly to the Lord of the harvest to send out laborers into his harvest" (Matt. 9:38). Are you burdened by the world's resistance to the gospel? "Pray . . . that the word of the Lord may speed ahead and be honored" (2 Thess. 3:1). Are you discouraged by spiritual opposition to the gospel? Remember that even the worst spiritual strongholds can be taken down by prayer (Mark 9:29). Are you worried that you won't be an effective witness if put to the test of adversity? Pray for strength that will allow you to escape the corruptions of the world and stand in integrity before God (Luke 21:36). Are you presently experiencing opposition or persecution for your witness? Pray for those who persecute and abuse you (Matt. 5:44; Luke 6:28). Do you wonder how God might use you to promote his peace in this world? One thing you can always do is "pray without ceasing" (1 Thess. 5:17). Whatever else we're called to do in the promotion of shalom, we can always, and at all times, engage in the transformative ministry of prayer.

Jonathan Edwards provides a fitting summary of how those who have received God's peace are to live and act and speak and pray and build and create in the world for the sake of peace:

> As you have not made yourself, so you were not made for yourself. You are neither the author nor the end of your own being. Nor is it you that uphold yourself in being, or that provide for

yourself, or that are dependent on yourself. There is another that hath made you, and preserves you, and provides for you, and on whom you are dependent: and He hath made you for himself, and for the good of your fellow creatures, and not only for yourself. He has placed before you higher and nobler ends than self, even the welfare of your fellowmen, and of society, and the interests of his kingdom; and for these you ought to labor and live, not only in time, but for eternity.[6]

A Closing Benediction

As we close this study on peace, it is my prayer that you will "labor and live" for the sake of shalom in a troubled world. But we who offer shalom need to taste it and live in the good of it as well. My desire for anyone finishing this book is that you will know the shalom of God in profound and life-shaping ways. Maybe the best way I can express my desire for how this book might affect your life is in the words of the Aaronic benediction in Numbers 6:24–26:

> The Lord bless you and keep you;
> the Lord make his face to shine upon you and be gracious
>   to you;
> the Lord lift up his countenance upon you and give you peace.

Appendix: Peace and . . .

THROUGHOUT THE PROCESS OF writing this book, thoughts and issues came to my mind that didn't seem to fit in any particular chapter. Rather than force them in where they didn't belong, I've included them here as short reflections on areas of life where peace needs to be worked out. There's no developed argument here, but maybe there are some things that can stir you to think more deeply about peace and how you can play a part to see it advance.

Political Action and Involvement Is an Arena for Peace, But It Does Not Create Peace

When Ronald Reagan was elected president in 1980, my Marxist passions were in overdrive. I truly believed we were going to be in a nuclear war within two years. A friend and I were so incensed at the results that we resorted to graffiti vandalism—painting a wall at our school with the words "Ronald Reagan, an actor in his greatest role." (I know it's not the cleverest thing to write, but we were angry, not clever.) Four years later, as a Christian, I voted for the Great Communicator to lead the Free World into a second term. So I've been passionate about politics on both ends of the spectrum.

Christians can get squirrely on politics. We don't always appreciate the difference between governing and politics. Government is a biblically sanctioned institution through which God operates for the restraint of sin and the outworking of his purpose in the earth. God raises up, tears down, and works through the governments of the earth (Ps. 47:8–9). Politics is the human process of organizing power in society. Christians have biblical responsibilities to the government (qualified submission, respect for leaders, etc.) that they don't have to the political world (see Matt. 22:21; Rom. 13:1–7; Titus 3:1; 1 Pet. 2:13–17). The things we find distasteful in politics—the compromise, the hype, the mudslinging, the dishonesty, the manipulation, etc.—simply reflect the way people acquire and use power in a fallen world. Christians in a free society need to be part of the political process in order to affect the governing process. The goals of politics and gospel, however, collide over power. Politics is about power in culture; the gospel is about the power of a kingdom not of this world. When Christians or the church link too closely to temporal political institutions or parties or causes, we submit the transcendent gospel to the fickle ways of a worldly system.

Yes, we should be participants in the governing process. Yes, we should understand and think hard in thoroughly biblical ways about the issues of our day. Yes, we can use the political structures and tools of our day to accomplish goals that promote justice and the moral environment that fosters peace. And yes, we can even participate in politics as politicians for the glory of God. But we are not of this world; the power we rely on cannot be generated from the grass roots up. It comes from the throne of God, and it has its own agenda. I love C. S. Lewis's summary of the Christian's best political activism: "He who converts his neighbor has performed the most practical Christian-political act of all."[1]

To Proclaim Peace but Live Like a Jerk
Doesn't Really Proclaim Peace

> Those of us who advocate the sacred cause of Christianity should be keenly aware that our being religious will never atone for our being disagreeable.[2]

These are the exasperated words of Hannah More, one of my spiritual heroes. More was an eighteenth-century English evangelical, close friend of William Wilberforce and John Newton. She was a key member of the Clapham Sect, the group of serious Christians who worked the strategy that ultimately overthrew the slave trade in England. But her impact for both the welfare of her society and salvation of souls extended well beyond abolition. She was a woman who traveled fluidly between the church and the culture. More was at home with nobility and statesmen, and with the common and the poor. She saw her share of controversy, at various times castigated by the cultural elite on the one hand and the established church on the other. What appalled Hannah More was the poor reputation that being "Christian" had in the culture, largely due to the arrogant and hypocritical behavior many professing Christians had displayed in the world in which she traveled. People who had simply been rubbed the wrong way by Christians needlessly opposed many good and charitable works. More's exasperated words above could speak just as relevantly in our day.

Brothers and sisters, someday we will be the Church Triumphant. But we are not that now, so we shouldn't act like we are. Those around us often tend to see us as the Church Troubled, the Church Bumbling and Stumbling, and the Church of Big Talk and Meager Results. The funny thing is, the world isn't looking for us to be all that remarkable. They think we're nuts anyway. They just want us to be genuine. They take notice when we are holy and humble, because that isn't something you can find anywhere else. If you are going to be an authentic witness, if your church is going to have a meaningful impact, follow the advice of David Wells:

> The Church has been most influential in those moments when its contrition reached down deeply into its soul, when in its known weakness it cried out to God from the depths, when it sought to live by his truth and on his terms, when it sought to proclaim that truth in its world, when it was willing to demand of itself that it live by that truth, when it sought above all else God in his grace and glory.[3]

Contextualization Is a Great Strategy but a Lousy Goal

Contextualization is a big word in missions these days. In the best sense it means that someone who wants to reach people in a certain cultural environment with the gospel will work to have it make sense in that environment. Contextualization fights against the historic mistakes of missions, which sought to build Western style churches in non-Western cultures. The impact was, in most cases, not lasting. There is some great contextualizing going on these days. When done well, the church looks to take the gospel into an unreached or underimpacted area by first becoming part of that community. Being real people who participate meaningfully in the lives and world of the people around us is not just great missions strategy, it is humble love.

But contextualization can undermine the true peace work of the gospel if it becomes a goal. There is a point to where God's people won't fit in any culture, because the message doesn't fit any culture. And people who receive that message will have to die to things they love about their culture in order to live in the culture of the Prince of Peace. A Christian individual or community who achieves full contextualization has probably given away some significant implication or application of the gospel. Vern Poythress makes a great point about the limits of contextualization in missions:

> In the name of contextualization, a missionary can make his version of the "gospel" fit in so well with the target culture that it accepts some of the false views and values in the culture: it becomes indistinguishable from the culture and does not challenge it at a fundamental level.[4]

If we're not thinking clearly about contextualization, what we really start driving for is cutting edge. We want to distance ourselves so far from whatever stereotype people have of Christianity that we identify more with the culture we are reaching than the culture we are representing. Cutting-edge relevance isn't really possible for a people who occupy themselves with eternal values. We're outsiders trying to do our business in somebody else's world.

Paul's contextualization strategy was pretty simple: "I have become all things to all people, that by all means I might save some" (1 Cor. 9:22). Not save *all*. No amount of contextualization could reach everyone. He could live at peace with "save some" because his goal wasn't numbers or success. "I do it all for the sake of the gospel" (9:23). Paul kept the strategy (contextualization) distinct from the goal (preaching the gospel). What makes the difference in reaching the lost is not our sameness. What makes the difference *is* the difference the gospel makes.

War Is Not a Pathway for the Gospel

This one is tough. It probably deserves its own chapter. I read a number of books by Christian pacifists and, to be honest, it was hard to disagree with a lot of what they said about war. Even secular pacifists had me thinking. Consider this comment from a secular peace theorist talking about the catastrophe of war in a world of complex problems:

> It is indeed paradoxical that in a time of unique danger and difficulty, the inhabitants of planet Earth waste their time, resources, and energy—as well as their lives—fighting among themselves and/or preparing to do so. Sadly there is nothing new in the human experience about recourse to war. What is new, however, is its profound inappropriateness: with the wolf at the door, we leap to our feet, grab a gun . . . and begin shooting at each other![5]

What I can say is this: war has never proven to be a pathway for the advance of the gospel. At times its effect has been necessary to restrain evil, restore legitimate national sovereignty, overthrow oppressive regimes, end tyrannical social ills, and combat the global cancer of terrorism. But it has never done any of these things without tremendous cost in lives, social destruction, and environmental waste. Historically, the people who tended to advocate war most were those who either had never personally experienced its decimation or had reason to profit by it. What we can never do is advocate war presumptively assuming we are right in doing so. History will judge that. And we cannot get behind war as a means of opening up a country or region for the gospel. God doesn't need us making war to do that. When war opens up a previously closed society, the gospel isn't the only thing that floods in. I recently read an article which surmised that the most influential thing left behind in Iraq with the withdrawal of troops in 2012 would be hip-hop culture.

The most valuable lesson I have gained in thinking about war and peace came from my dad, who passed away two years ago. He was a military man; he had been on a bomb disposal unit in a devastated Europe following World War II and had done a stint in Korea as well. The greatest material gift he left me was a World War II era M1 carbine paratrooper rifle, which I will always treasure. The greatest moral gift he gave me was to learn how to think about war. He helped me see that I can never be a pacifist, because my country does need to use its resources, including its military, to protect those in the world who cannot protect themselves. But he was under no delusion that every military action has that goal or achieves that end. He could be critical of military means and rationale if he saw it as morally questionable or unwise. I've learned that from him as well. So my support for any military actions on the part of my government must be guided by a biblically informed conscience. What particularly engages me is the story of the soldier, the individual who commits himself or herself to a duty on my behalf that could, and often does, come at the cost of life. This is where I'm grateful for my dad. He taught me to honor the soldier but love the peace that brings him home.

Social Action Can Be a Ministry of the Church, But It Can Never Be the Mission of the Church

In chapter 10 I talked about the pursuit of shalom as part of the lasting mandate of God's people. We focused on the rule of social justice in this pursuit of peace. But there are some specific applications of this that I want to focus on here.

I've been reading a lot these days about "externally focused churches" and "cross-domain collaboration." These concepts are intriguing. Social justice, the traditional purview of the liberal wing of Christianity, is being taken up by gospel-preaching churches. They emphasize the need to be externally focused—to go into an area, particularly an urban area, looking for where the church can meet the needs of the community. We're not talking just charity here. We're talking community involvement and engagement through working with the poor, community development, and social action.

Connected to this fresh passion for social justice is a strategic vision to partner with existing social service and community development groups across and beyond religious lines. It's an intriguing idea. Why reinvent the wheel of community impact when experienced and proven work is already being done in the area? And what better way to make the church a relevant player in the community than by putting it on the front lines of the practical needs of people it is reaching out to? The author of a recent book advocating a strong social justice stance for churches says this: "My hope is that God would open our eyes more and more to the needs of our community. And that we would see it as the church's responsibility to lead the charge."[6]

What's refreshing is that most of the leading "externally focused" people preach the gospel. What remains to be seen is what happens to the church, and ultimately to the message, if the church leads the charge into areas where its help is needed but its message is prohibited. When the church as an institution links with other institutions, it must compromise on how things get done, and by whom they are done. It finds itself linked with organizations and movements that can change or deteriorate. Then when the church reassesses its community investment or pulls back, the goodwill accrued can easily be washed away in a flood of criticism by those affected by its departure.

There are genuine risks in seeking to promote peace through linkage to social services. My sense is that churches should encourage individual Christians to proactively engage in meeting the needs of their local communities. It should support and pray for these individuals in what can be discouraging labor. Churches as institutions can look for opportunities to be part of the building of the community and the meeting of its needs in ways that don't co-opt the resources that should be committed to the discipling of their people for the sake of mission. Ultimately, I agree with evangelist J. Mack Stiles: "Caring for others represents the gospel, it upholds the gospel, it points to the gospel, it's an implication of the gospel, but it is not the gospel, and it is not equal to the gospel."[7]

The Arts Culture Is an Unreached Mission Field Ripe for the Gospel of Peace

This may be an odd topic to end on but it's a personal passion. I'm not an artist, but as I've studied the topic of peace, I've been struck by how much the realm of peace and the expressions of art intersect. Arts came into existence as an expression of humanity's image-bearing capacity. God the Creator has made us image bearers with the capacity to create. He created from nothing; we create from interaction with the world he created. It is in that connection between the shalom of God and the sin of man that artistic expression now finds its spark. Consider the words of theologian Leland Ryken:

> The arts are humankind's most accurate record of their affirmations and denials, their longings and fears. The arts are a picture of the kind of world people aspire to create and of the fallen realities that keep thwarting those aspirations. . . . The arts express how the human race has felt about the facts of existence. Art is the record of people's involvement with life. It deals not simply with the facts of life but with things as they matter to people.[8]

In spite of this deep theological well from which art emerges, there may be no area of culture where Christians are so irrelevant today as in the world of the arts. We need a meaningful arts missiology if we are going to engage our culture where it is being most profoundly shaped. Christians should cultivate an appreciation of art in its best and most relevant forms because art communicates something of our capacity as image bearers of God. But art also tells us where our culture is going like no other human endeavor. Christians with artistic gifts should boldly do their work as artists with passion and excellence because they have a vantage point that is truly distinct. The church should be in meaningful conversation with the arts because there are lost artists who are cultural light-years from the church, who may never hear the message of shalom or see it lived out by anyone else if we are not somehow intersecting with their world.

Christian artists and churches have to forge a workable partnership that respects how the agendas of both can work in redemptive tension. I have the privilege of working pastorally with artists in a group called The Gathering. Their boundless patience with me has taught me much about grace. In the process I have learned as a pastor to think and theologize in fresh ways. I'm much indebted to them for this gift. We're not an arts church, and may never be in the way people sometimes picture that kind of thing. But we want our artists to have a place where they can be discipled as Christians and encouraged as creators. It's an education in the unfamiliar for us all. But we believe it is shalom work of the best kind, and we're committed to doing it together.

> Now may the Lord of peace himself give you peace at all times in every way. The Lord be with you all. (2 Thess. 3:16)

Notes

Introduction
1. Of the twenty-two epistles in the New Testament, only Hebrews, James, 1 John, and 3 John do not begin with this greeting.

Chapter 1: Peace, and the Problem with It
1. As quoted by Anthony B. Robinson in "Articles of Faith: Consumerism Is a Greedy Society's Religion," *Seattle Pi.com*, February, 8, 2008, http://www.seattlepi.com/default/article/Articles-of-Faith-Consumerism-is-a-greedy-1263940.php#ixzz1MoyXRxrx.

2. See "High Cost of Low Status: Feeling Powerless Leads to Expensive Purchases," *Science Daily*, June 26, 2008, http://www.sciencedaily.com/releases/2008/06/080625193859.htm.

Chapter 2: Is True Peace Possible?
1. Cornelius Plantinga Jr., *Not the Way It's Supposed to Be: A Breviary of Sin* (Grand Rapids, MI: Eerdmans, 1995), 10.

2. Timothy Keller, *Generous Justice: How God's Grace Makes Us Just* (New York: Dutton, 2010), 173.

3. Herman Bavinck, *Our Reasonable Faith* (Grand Rapids, MI: Eerdmans, 1977), 260–61.

4. "As in Study 1, nonaffiliates (atheist/agnostic or 'none') reported more anger toward God than affiliates. . . . We had also proposed that the concept of anger toward God would extend to some atheists and agnostics, and results supported this prediction. Compared with religious affiliates, nonaffiliates (including atheists, agnostics, and those reporting 'none' for religion) reported greater anger toward God in terms of lifetime frequency (Study 3) and intensity (Studies 2–4). Granted, these findings were not straightforward to interpret, particularly in Study 3, where participants who did not believe in God were asked to speculate about their responses if God did exist. Nonetheless, these findings suggest that researchers and clinicians might miss important information if they restrict their work on anger toward God to religious affiliates and professed believers. Not only may some atheists and agnostics have anger toward God as part of their religious/spiritual history, but some may still have anger focused on images of a hypothetical God. In future work, it will be valuable to examine causal connections: Does anger toward God promote decreased belief? Does doubt make anger toward God more likely? Or does some third variable—perhaps a cognitive style or personality factor—explain the association? Another important task will be to pinpoint the contribution of anger toward God (and other forms of spiritual struggle), relative to the roles of socialization or intellectual questioning, as predictors of nonbelief or disaffiliation," "Anger toward God: Social-cognitive predictors, prevalence, and links with adjustment to bereavement and cancer," Julie J. Exline, Crystal L. Park, M. Smyth, Michael P. Carey, *Journal of Personality and Social Psychology*, 100, no. 1 (January 2011): 129–48, doi: 10.1037/a0021716, http://psycnet.apa.org/journals/psp/100/1/129.html.

5. D. Martyn Lloyd-Jones, quoted in Iain Murray, *Lloyd-Jones: Messenger of Grace* (Edinburgh, UK: Banner of Truth Trust, 2008), 71–72.

6. Keller, *Generous Justice*, 176–77.

7. Walter Brueggeman, *Peace* (St. Louis, MO: Chalice Press, 2001), 60.

8. John Bright, *A History of Israel*, 3rd ed. (Philadelphia: Westminster Press, 1981), 358.

Chapter 3: The Prince of Peace
1. Felix Geyer, *Sociology of Alienation, International Encyclopedia of the Social and Behavioral Sciences*, ed. Paul Baltes and Neil Smelser (London: Elsevier, 2001), 391.

2. Jimmy Carter, "Crisis of Confidence," *American Experience* (televised speech, July 15, 1979), http://www.pbs.org/wgbh/americanexperience/features/primary-resources/carter-crisis/.

3. Karl Marx, *Critique of Hegel's Philosophy of Right* (Cambridge, UK: University of Cambridge Press, 1970), 131, Google Books, http://books.google.com/books?id=uxg4AAAAIAAJ&pg=PA129&lpg=PA129&dq=A+Contribution+to+the+Critique+of+Hegel%E2%80%99s+Philosophy+of+Right+Introduction&source=bl&ots=v7x4iOoBux&sig=9reUnR32ao3tmS5_gefXooEW2C4&hl=en&sa=X&ei=5OMpT_-8N8Xm0gGr3P29Cg&ved=0CE4Q6AEwBg#v=onepage&q=A%20Contribution%20to%20the%20Critique%20of%20Hegel%E2%80%99s%20Philosophy%20of%20Right%20Introduction&f=false.

4. John Flavel, "The Fountain of Life Opened Up," Christian Classics Ethereal Library, sermon 12, 124, http://www.ccel.org/ccel/flavel/fountain.pdf.

5. Robert Murray McCheyne and Andrew A. Bonar, *Memoir and Remains of the Rev. Robert Murray McCheyne* (Edinburgh; London, UK: Oliphant Anderson & Ferrier, 1894), Libronix Digital Library System, 330.

6. Graham Cole, *God the Peacemaker: How Atonement Brings Shalom* (Nottingham, UK: Apollos, 2009), 178.

7. Encyclopedia of Marxism, s.v. "alienation," http://www.marxists.org/glossary/terms/a/l.htm.

8. Jerry Bridges, *The Gospel for Real Life: Turn to the Liberating Power of the Cross . . . Every Day* (Colorado Springs, CO: NavPress, 2002), 94–95.

9. Ideas from Ted Kober, "Forget Not All His Benefits" (lecture, Sovereign Grace Pastors Conference, November 10, 2011).

10. Thabiti Anyabwile, "The Supremacy of Christ in Ethnic Distinctions and Identities," in *For the Fame of God's Name: Essays in Honor of John Piper* (Wheaton, IL: Crossway, 2010), 301.

11. Charles Spurgeon, *According to Promise*, Grace-ebooks edition, 53–54, http://grace-ebooks.com/library/Charles%20Spurgeon/CHS_According%20to%20Promise.PDF.

Chapter 4: Peace and Stress

1. Wayne Dyer, *Ten Secrets for Success and Inner Peace* (Carlsbad, CA: Hay House, 2001), 58.

2. Jonathan Edwards, *The Works of Jonathan Edwards*, "The Peace Which Christ Gives His True Followers," vol. 25, *Sermons and Discourses, 1743–1758*, ed. Wilson H. Kimnach (New Haven, CT: Yale University Press, 2006), 548.

3. B. B. Warfield, *Faith and Life* (Edinburgh, UK: Banner of Truth Trust, 1990), 329, 339.

4. William Hendriksen, *Philippians, Colossians, and Philemon* (Grand Rapids, MI: Baker, 1979), 196.

5. Quoted in Rabbi Aharon Lichtenstein, *Henry More: The Rational Theology of a Cambridge Platonist* (Cambridge, MA: Cambridge University Press, 1962), 100. Lichtenstein's source for this quote in the footnotes is Leonard Lyons, *Boston Herald*, January 2, 1957, 23.

6. J. Alec Motyer, *The Message of Philippians*, The Bible Speaks Today, ed. John Stott (Downers Grove, MI: InterVarsity Press, 1988), 208.

7. Billy Graham, interview with Greta Van Susteren, *Fox News.com*, December 20, 2010. See Erin Roach, "Billy Graham, in TV interview, Reflects: 'My Time Is Limited,'" *Baptist Press*, December 21, 2010, http://www.bpnews.net/bpnews.asp?id=34303.

8. Author Tim Challies defines discernment as "the skill of understanding and applying God's word with the purpose of separating truth from error and right from wrong," Tim Challies, *The Discipline of Spiritual Discernment* (Wheaton, IL: Crossway, 2007), 61.

9. A. W. Tozer, *The Quotable Tozer*, comp. Harry Verploegh (Camp Hill, PA: Christian Publications, 1994), 9.

10. G. Walter Hansen, *The Letter to the Philippians*, The Pillar New Testament Commentary, (Grand Rapids, MI: Eerdmans, 2009), 299.

Chapter 5: Peace and Anxiety

1. Elyse Fitzpatrick, *Overcoming Fear, Worry, and Anxiety* (Eugene, OR: Harvest House, 2001), 14.

2. Edward T. Welch, *Running Scared: Fear, Worry, and the God of Rest* (Greensboro, NC: New Growth Press, 2007), 25.

3. NIMH, "Brain Activity Patterns in Anxiety-Prone People Suggest Deficits in Handling Fear," February 9, 2011, http://www.nimh.nih.gov/science-news/2011/brain-activity-patterns-in-anxiety-prone-people-suggest-deficits-in-handling-fear.shtml.

4. For easily understandable descriptions of the various types of diagnosable anxiety disorders and their current treatments see the National Institute of Mental Health website for "Anxiety Disorders," http://www.nimh.nih.gov/health/topics/anxiety-disorders/index.shtml.

5. Jerry Bridges, *The Practice of Godliness* (Colorado Springs, CO: NavPress, 1991), 27.

6. Also in Luke 12:22–34. Some commentators believe that this passage is not a parallel

to Matthew 6 but actually another occasion where Jesus taught the same basic principles, with slightly different emphases.

7. Harry S. Truman, "We Must Not Fail or Falter" (speech, lighting of the National Community Christmas Tree, Washington, DC, December 24, 1945), http://www.ibiblio.org/pha/policy/post-war/1945-12-24b.html.

8. John R. W. Stott, *The Message of the Sermon on the Mount*, The Bible Speaks Today (Leicester, UK: Inter-Varsity Press, 1978), 19.

9. *New International Dictionary of Biblical Theology*, vol. 1, ed. Colin Brown (Grand Rapids, MI: Zondervan, 1986), s.vv. "care," "anxiety," 277.

10. This concept is taken from David Powlison, "Don't Worry," *The Journal of Biblical Counseling* (Winter 2003): 58.

11. John Piper, *Future Grace: The Purifying Power of the Promises of God* (Sisters, OR: Multnomah, 1995), 54.

12. From "Humiliation," *The Valley of Vision*, ed. Arthur G. Bennett (Edinburgh, UK: Banner of Truth Trust, 2002), 142.

13. Thomas Watson, *The Godly Man's Picture* (Edinburgh, UK: Banner of Truth Trust, 1999), 225–26.

14. Richard McNally, quoted in Stacey Burling, "Torment's Intensive Carer: Penetrating Methods Make Edna Foa a Leader in Treating Post-traumatic Stress," *Philadelphia Inquirer*, January 2, 2011.

15. John Flavel, *The Mystery of Providence* (Edinburgh, UK: Banner of Truth Trust, 2002), 183.

Chapter 6: Peace and Grief

1. J. I. Packer, *A Grief Sanctified: Through Sorrow to Eternal Hope* (Wheaton, IL: Crossway, 2002), 9.

2. C. S. Lewis, *A Grief Observed* (New York: Harper Collins, 2001), 10.

3. Bar Scott, *The Present Giver: A Memoir* (Glenford, NY: ALM Books, 2011), Kindle edition, part 3, "Happy Mom."

4. Lewis, *A Grief Observed*, 33.

5. Nicholas Wolterstorff, *Lament for a Son* (Grand Rapids, IL: Eerdmans, 1987), Kindle edition, locations 60, 153.

6. Gregory of Nyssa, as quoted by Hans Boersma in "Hope-Bridled Grief: Discovering in Gregory of Nyssa a Christian Discipline of Grief," *First Things*, January 2012, http://www.firstthings.com/article/2011/12/hope-bridled-grief.

7. See chapter 2 for a further discussion about the benefits of the atonement for us and our salvation.

8. Some commentators would restrict this beatitude for mourning over sin, which is certainly included. But the structure of the beatitudes and the fact that this language ties back into rich Old Testament imagery seems to argue for a mourning in a broken, fallen world, of which guilt in sin is a fundamental but not exclusive burden.

9. Wolterstorff, *Lament for a Son*, location 143.

10. Paul David Tripp, "When Grief Enters Your Door," *The Journal of Biblical Counseling* (Winter 2005): 8.

11. Nancy Guthrie, excerpt from *Holding on to Hope: A Pathway through Suffering to the Heart of God*, NancyGuthrie.com, http://www.nancyguthrie.com/books/hoh_excerpts.php.

Chapter 7: Peace and Depression

1. Elizabeth Wurtzel, *Prozac Nation: Young and Depressed in America* (Boston: Houghton Mifflin, 1994), n.p.

2. Dan G. Blazer, "The Depression Epidemic," *Christianity Today*, March 2009, 24.

3. Edward T. Welch, *Depression: A Stubborn Darkness* (Winston-Salem, NC: Punch Press, 2004), 55–56.

4. John Newton, *Letters of John Newton* (Edinburgh, UK: Banner of Truth Trust, 2007), 395.

5. See William A. VanGemeren on the setting of Psalm 23 in *Psalms*, The Expositor's Bible Commentary (Grand Rapids, MI: Zondervan, 1998), 5:214.

6. Welch, *Depression*, 53.

7. D. Martyn Lloyd-Jones, *Spiritual Depression* (Grand Rapids, MI: Eerdmans, 2003), 44.

8. Timothy S. Laniak, *Shepherds After My Own Heart* (Leichester, UK: Apollos Press, 2006), 112.

9. As quoted by Joshua Wolf Shenk in *Lincoln's Melancholy: How Depression Challenged a President and Fueled His Greatness* (New York: Houghton Mifflin, 2005), 62.

10. As quoted by Lewis Drummond in *Spurgeon: Prince of Preachers* (Grand Rapids, MI: Kregel, 1992), 435.

11. Sinclair B. Ferguson, *Deserted by God* (Grand Rapids, MI: Baker, 1993), 48.
12. Ibid.
13. Phillip Keller, *A Shepherd Looks at Psalm 23*, from the compilation *Phillip Keller: The Inspirational Writings* (Edison, NJ: Inspiration Press, 1993), 113.

Chapter 8: Peace and Conflict

1. David Powlison, "The Sufficiency of Scripture to Diagnose and Cure Souls," *The Journal of Biblical Counseling* (Spring 2005): 12.
2. The Arbinger Institute, *The Anatomy of Peace: Resolving the Heart of Conflict* (San Francisco: Barrett-Koehler, 2006), xx.
3. Alfred Poirier, *The Peacemaking Pastor* (Grand Rapids, MI: Baker, 2007), 139.
4. Ken Sande, *The Peacemaker* (Grand Rapids, MI Baker, 1994), 118–19.
5. Poirer, *Peacemaker Pastor*, 150.
6. Cornelius Plantinga, personal notes from a message on forgiveness, given at the Living Faith 2004 conference sponsored by the Christian Counseling and Education Foundation.

Chapter 9: Peace and God's People

1. Graham Goldsworthy, *Gospel and Wisdom* in *The Goldsworthy Trilogy* (Waynesboro, GA: Paternoster Press, 2000), 490.
2. J. A. Motyer, *The Message of James: The Tests of Faith*, The Bible Speaks Today (Leicester, UK: InterVarsity Press, 1985), 135.
3. Peter H. Davids, *The Epistle of James*, New International Greek Testament Commentary (Grand Rapids, MI: Eerdmans, 1982), 151.
4. Bertrand Russell, *On Education, Especially in Early Childhood* (London: George Allen & Unwin, 1926), 59.
5. John F. Kennedy, "Declaration of Honorary Citizen of United States of America April 9, 1963," WinstonChurchill.org, http://www.winstonchurchill.org/learn/speeches/speeches-of-winston-churchill/125-united-states-citizen.
6. J. Gresham Machen, *Christianity and Liberalism* (Grand Rapids, MI: Eerdmans, 1922), 180.

Chapter 10: Peace and My World

1. Bruce Milne, *The Message of John: Here Is Your King! With Study Guide*, The Bible Speaks Today (Leicester, UK; Downers Grove, IL: Inter-Varsity Press, 1993), 296.
2. Timothy Keller, *Generous Justice: How God's Grace Makes Us Just* (New York: Dutton, 2010), 18.
3. For arguments in favor of application to all believers, see Stanley E. Porter, "Peace, Reconciliation," *Dictionary of Paul and His Letters*, ed. Gerald F. Hawthorne and Ralph P. Martin (Downers Grove, IL: InterVarsity Press, 1993), 695; and Murray J. Harris, *The Second Epistle to the Corinthians*, New International Greek Testament Commentary (Grand Rapids, MI: Eerdmans, 2005), 435. See Paul W. Barnett, *The Second Epistle to the Corinthians*, New International Commentary on the New Testament (Grand Rapids, MI: Eerdmans, 1997), 304; and Ralph P. Martin, *2 Corinthians*, Word Biblical Commentary (Nashville, TN: Thomas Nelson, 1986), 148, for arguments that limit this passage to problems specifically being addressed by Paul regarding his apostolic role in Corinth.
4. Kevin DeYoung and Greg Gilbert, *What Is the Mission of the Church?* (Wheaton, IL: Crossway, 2011), 229.
5. Andy Crouch, *Culture Making: Rediscovering Our Creative Calling* (Downers Grove, IL: InterVarsity Press, 2008), 200.
6. Jonathan Edwards, *Charity and Its Fruits* (Edinburgh, UK: Banner of Truth Trust, 1996), 180–81.

Appendix: Peace and . . .

1. C. S. Lewis, *God in the Dock* (Grand Rapids, MI:. Eerdmans, 1970), 199.
2. Hannah More, *Religion of the Heart* (Orleans, MA: Paraclete Press, 1993), 148.
3. David F. Wells, *Above All Earthly Pow'rs: Christ in a Postmodern World* (Grand Rapids, MI: Eerdmans, 2005), 315–16.
4. Vern Sheridan Poythress, *Redeeming Sociology: A God-Centered Approach* (Wheaton, IL: Crossway, 2011), 140.
5. David Barash, ed., *Approaches to Peace* (New York: Oxford University Press, 2000), 3.
6. Brandon Hatmaker, commenting on his book *Barefoot Church*, on Brandon Hatmaker .com, http://brandonhatmaker.com/books-reviews.htm.
7. J. Mack Stiles, *Marks of the Messenger* (Downers Grove, IL: IVP, 2010), 69.
8. Leland Ryken, *The Liberated Imagination: Thinking Christianly About the Arts* (Colorado Springs, CO: Waterbrook, 1989), 265–66.

Scripture Index